How Not to Be Human

How Not to Be Human

The Inhumanist Philosophy of Robinson Jeffers

Matthew Calarco

ANTHEM PRESS

Anthem Press
An imprint of Wimbledon Publishing Company
www.anthempress.com

This edition first published in UK and USA 2026
by ANTHEM PRESS
75–76 Blackfriars Road, London SE1 8HA, UK
or PO Box 9779, London SW19 7ZG, UK
and
244 Madison Ave #116, New York, NY 10016, USA

First published in the UK and USA by Anthem Press in 2024

© 2026 Matthew Calarco

The author asserts the moral right to be identified as the author of this work.

All rights reserved. Without limiting the rights under copyright reserved above, no part of this publication may be reproduced, stored or introduced into a retrieval system, or transmitted, in any form or by any means (electronic, mechanical, photocopying, recording or otherwise), without the prior written permission of both the copyright owner and the above publisher of this book.

British Library Cataloguing-in-Publication Data
A catalogue record for this book is available from the British Library.

Library of Congress Control Number: 2026931058

ISBN-13: 978-1-83999-947-5 (Pbk)
ISBN-10: 1-83999-947-0 (Pbk)

This title is also available as an eBook.

CONTENTS

Preface — vii

Abbreviations of Works by Robinson Jeffers — ix

Introduction: Between Poetry and Philosophy — 1

1. Evil — 19
2. Saviors — 35
3. Cosmos — 47
4. Human — 63
5. Value — 81

Conclusion: Inhumanism — 99

Suggestions for Further Reading — 107

Index — 109

PREFACE

This book is addressed primarily to readers who are new to the poetry of Robinson Jeffers. In particular, I hope it finds readers who are interested in recent debates about the status of "the human" and who might wish to learn something about what Jeffers can offer these ongoing conversations. I make the case in this book that Jeffers is an essential precursor for contemporary discussions about inhumanism and that his radical non-anthropocentrism remains deeply relevant for work being done in the environmental humanities, environmental philosophy, animal studies, and related fields.

Advanced scholars in Jeffers studies who find their way to this work will encounter much that is familiar but a few new themes and ideas as well. With my focus on inhumanism, I am not trying of course to break new ground. This is a central—perhaps *the* central—philosophical and spiritual concern of Jeffers's work, and many scholars before me have examined it. So, too, many of the poems I discuss in this book have been expertly analyzed by previous and present generations of literary critics, and I am much indebted to their scholarship. At the same time, the heavy emphasis I give to the philosophical and theoretical dimensions of Jeffers's work cuts against the grain of some of the existing scholarship, and specialists will readily note the ways in which I push back against certain established readings of Jeffers. Scholars will, I hope, also appreciate how my approach to understanding philosophy as a way of life (as opposed to, say, a mode of discourse focused primarily on making arguments and defending metaphysical and epistemological theses) allows the philosophical dimensions of Jeffers's work to be differently illuminated.

Given that this book is primarily intended for the former (general and non-specialist) audience rather than the latter (scholarly and specialist), I have avoided cluttering the main body of the work with discussions of the secondary scholarship. I have instead provided footnotes in various places pointing readers to secondary works that have proved useful for my own analyses. I have also included "Suggestions for Further Reading" at the end of the book for readers who wish to delve further into Jeffers's poetry and the substantial body of scholarship on his work.

ABBREVIATIONS OF WORKS BY ROBINSON JEFFERS

The standard scholarly edition of Jeffers's work is *The Collected Poetry of Robinson Jeffers* (listed below as CP). I have cited these volumes throughout. Tim Hunt's excellent anthology of Jeffers's work, *The Selected Poetry of Robinson Jeffers* (listed below as SP), is widely available and affordable. If a poem or prose work I discuss is reprinted in SP, I also cite this volume for the convenience of readers who might not have access to CP.

CL 1   *The Collected Letters of Robinson Jeffers, with Selected Letters of Una Jeffers*, vol. 1, 1890–1930, ed. James Karman (Stanford: Stanford University Press, 2009)

CL 2   *The Collected Letters of Robinson Jeffers, with Selected Letters of Una Jeffers*, vol. 2, 1931–1939, ed. James Karman (Stanford: Stanford University Press, 2011)

CL 3   *The Collected Letters of Robinson Jeffers, with Selected Letters of Una Jeffers*, vol. 3, 1940–1962, ed. James Karman (Stanford: Stanford University Press, 2015)

CP 1   *The Collected Poetry of Robinson Jeffers*, vol. 1, 1920–1928, ed., Tim Hunt (Stanford: Stanford University Press, 1988)

CP 2   *The Collected Poetry of Robinson Jeffers*, vol. 2, 1928–1938, ed., Tim Hunt (Stanford: Stanford University Press, 1989)

CP 3   *The Collected Poetry of Robinson Jeffers*, vol. 3, 1938–1962, ed., Tim Hunt (Stanford: Stanford University Press, 1991)

CP 4   *The Collected Poetry of Robinson Jeffers*, vol. 4, Poetry 1903–1920, Prose, and Unpublished Writings, ed., Tim Hunt (Stanford: Stanford University Press, 2000)

CP 5   *The Collected Poetry of Robinson Jeffers*, vol. 5, Textual Evidence and Commentary, ed., Tim Hunt (Stanford: Stanford University Press, 2001)

SP   *The Selected Poetry of Robinson Jeffers*, ed. Tim Hunt (Stanford: Stanford University Press, 2001)

INTRODUCTION: BETWEEN POETRY AND PHILOSOPHY

This is a book about what the poet Robinson Jeffers would have described as "rock-solid themes" (CP 3, 35; SP, 567). It is about who we are and how we fit into the big scheme of things. It is about living and dying well in an era of cultural decline and ecological degradation. It is about dealing with the difficulties of existence and determining which things should be of paramount value and importance in our lives. Both Jeffers's poetry and his life as a whole were centered around these rock-solid themes—issues and questions that are as ancient as our oldest extant literature yet as fresh and as pressing for us today as they have been for any previous age.

If, as Charles Baudelaire suggests, modernity is marked by a turn toward "the ephemeral, the fugitive, and the contingent,"[1] then the themes that form the focus of this book and Jeffers's poetic reflections on them must be understood as being distinctively and resolutely *non*modern in nature. Jeffers sought to admit into his poetry only material that spoke to (relatively) permanent realities (CP 4, 391; SP, 714), matters that would be of importance to people who might happen to read them one hundred and even a thousand years hence (CP 4, 422–27; SP, 723–28). It is perhaps this focus on perennial matters that has made his work (which entered its mature phase nearly a full century ago now) newly relevant for those of us who live in the so-called Anthropocene, an age in which planetary conditions have forced us to reckon anew with intellectual and existential battles we might have once thought we had been spared.[2]

Although Jeffers engaged in a wide variety of pursuits and practices throughout his life, he was, perhaps above all else, a poet. Besides the prose

---

1 Charles Baudelaire, *The Painter of Modern Life and Other Essays*, trans. and ed. Jonathan Mayne (New York: Phaidon, 1965), 13.
2 I discuss the concept of the Anthropocene in relation to Jeffers's work in more detail in Chapter 4.

contained in his letters, prefaces to various volumes, and occasional essays, his published writing is made up almost exclusively of poetic verse. His poems took several forms, from tightly written lyrics to full-length tragic dramas to sprawling, epic-style narratives that run well over one-hundred pages in length. His collected works fill four large volumes, the by-product of a lifetime spent writing, reading, and reflecting on matters that were of profound importance both to him and to his substantial readership. To engage Jeffers's work charitably, then, one must read him first and foremost (and in line with T. S. Eliot's dictum[3]) *as* a poet. Part of the aim of this book is to invite and encourage you, the reader, to engage in this task—for Jeffers's poetic voice and overall project are undoubtedly among the most remarkable and powerful of his generation.

For those readers who sometimes find poetry off-putting or impenetrable, I should note that one need not be a professional literary critic to enjoy and profit from Jeffers's work. I am myself not a professional literary critic; my background and training are in philosophy. Accordingly, my approach to Jeffers's poetry will be rather different from that of professional critics and the bulk of Jeffers scholars, most of whom are trained in literary theory. This group of specialists has been primarily engaged in recent years with assessing Jeffers's place (or lack thereof) in the canon of modernist poetry.[4] Ranked early in his career among such luminaries as T. S. Eliot and Ezra Pound—poets who have since gained a secure place in the poetic canon—Jeffers's reputation among scholars declined in the following years and has undergone periodic revivals and declines in more recent years. The time is now ripe, these scholars suggest, to reconsider whether Jeffers's poetry has been given its proper due. This is undoubtedly an important question, but it is not one that will occupy my attention here. Rather, I am interested in certain philosophical aspects of Jeffers's verse and will approach his body of work primarily (but not exclusively) from that angle.

Historically, the relationship between poetry and philosophy has been close and productive at certain times, contentious and hostile at others. In the Western philosophical tradition, some of the earliest philosophers actually wrote their works using standard poetic devices and forms (as we find in Parmenides's fragments, which are written in Homeric hexameters and

---

[3] "When we are considering poetry we must consider it primarily as poetry and not another thing" (T. S. Eliot, *The Sacred Wood: Essays on Poetry and Criticism* [London: Methuen & Co., 1920], viii).

[4] For a helpful introduction to these debates, see Tim Hunt, "Robinson Jeffers: The Modern Poet as Antimodernist," in *Critical Essays on Robinson Jeffers*, ed. James Karman (Boston, MA: G. K. Hall & Co., 1990), 245–52.

report the words of a goddess, and in Empedocles's fragments, which are also written in hexameters and address a Muse).[5] This friendly relationship continued into the classical Roman era with figures such as Lucretius (an important influence on Jeffers), who elaborated his Epicurean philosophy by way of a long, six-book poem written in hexameters, and it has persisted into more recent times with philosophers like Friedrich Nietzsche, who himself occasionally wrote in verse form and engaged a vast body of ancient and contemporary poetry in his philosophical reflections. Such indebtedness and general amicability to poetic thought is clearly evident as well in the work of a number of formidable and influential contemporary philosophers, including Martin Heidegger, Gilles Deleuze, Jacques Derrida, Alain Badiou, Hélène Cixous,[6] Luce Irigaray, and Julia Kristeva.[7] The examples could be multiplied here, but suffice it to note that philosophers have long maintained an affirmative and productive engagement with poets.

Because the relationship between these two discursive registers has often been so close, there have also been times where philosophers have felt it necessary to sharply distinguish philosophy from poetry. This process of sifting and distinguishing between the two has sometimes turned antagonistic and issued in what Plato calls the "ancient quarrel" between poetry and philosophy.[8] In Book 10 of his *Republic*, Plato—or, rather, the figure of Socrates as portrayed in the *Republic*—takes up this quarrel on behalf of philosophy and seeks to determine if poetry has a place in his ideal republic. Poetry would only be welcome in that space, Socrates maintains, if its verse contains true things and encourages its listeners to become virtuous—the assumption being, of course, that truth and virtue are the primary and defining features of the philosophical life, that such a way of life is only possible if virtue is believed to be better than vice, and that such philosophical concerns and commitments are the measure against which all other facets of social life should be assessed. Poetry, especially Homeric and tragic poetry, seem to challenge these philosophical assumptions and commitments in certain ways. Its storylines revolve

---

5 Poetry and philosophy have also had close and complex relationships in a variety of non-Western traditions; the relationship between the *Vedas* and the *Upanishads* is but one important example.
6 It is reported that Cixous prepared a work on Jeffers's poetry, but to my knowledge this project has never been published. See Hélène Cixous and Mireille Calle-Gruber, *Hélène Cixous, Rootprints: Memory and Life Writing*, trans. Eric Prenowitz (New York: Routledge, 1997), 210.
7 For more on these connections, see the essays collected in Ranjan Ghosh, ed., *Philosophy and Poetry: Continental Perspectives* (New York: Columbia University Press, 2019).
8 Plato, *Republic*, trans. C. D. C. Reeve (Indianapolis: Hackett, 2004), 607b.

around heroes and figures whose character is often questionable; and the myths they purvey often depict the gods engaging in unjust and immoral behaviors. As with other philosophers like Xenophanes and Heraclitus, the Socrates of the *Republic* finds poetry generally lacking when measured against his philosophical ideals and hence sees little use for it in the project of constituting an ideal *polis*.[9] That this quarrel was already ancient nearly 2,500 years ago in Plato's time suggests that philosophy and poetry, despite sometimes occupying shared terrain, have never been perfectly aligned pursuits and often promote conflicting values, differing views of the world, and opposing senses of the place of human beings in the larger cosmic scheme.

In my reading of Jeffers's work, I will be mindful of certain distinctions between poetry and philosophy, distinctions that reflect my own concerns in the present work and that are also marked by Jeffers himself. That said, I do not believe there is an insuperable line demarcating philosophy from poetry. Poets often deal with themes that are of direct interest to philosophers, and it would be injudicious for philosophers to ignore careful thinking concerning such themes just because it derives from outside their ranks. In this vein, my engagement with Jeffers forthrightly assumes that his poetry has clear implications and indisputable importance for philosophy.

I should note, though, that my understanding of what constitutes philosophy might differ from what some readers take that term to mean. Philosophy today is typically viewed and practiced as a strictly academic discipline structured around a series of specialized and highly refined debates in such fields as metaphysics, epistemology, logic, ethics, and so on. Philosophical debates of this academic variety are usually carried out in academic publications and in technical language generally inaccessible to non-specialists. While these technical philosophical debates and discussions do have some value, contributing to them is not what drives my engagement with Jeffers. Here, my concerns are much more "existential" in nature, which is to say, they bear on how all of us—not just professional philosophers—live our lives, and they revolve around the sorts of "rock-solid" themes mentioned in the opening paragraph of this introduction. These sorts of themes belong to philosophy understood not as a narrow academic discipline open to a handful of specialists but as

---

9 At least, such is the conclusion that the surface layer of the text suggests. Although I will not elaborate on this point here, I actually believe Plato's engagement with poetry is considerably more complex, more ironic, and more conflicted than the brief sketch of the "ancient quarrel" I have provided would indicate. For a recent collection of essays on this issue, see Pierre Destrée and Fritz-Gregor Herrmann, eds., *Plato and the Poets* (Boston: Brill, 2011).

the sustained pursuit and formation of a way of life open to all who wish to pursue it.

Philosophy as the practice of a way of life has antecedents in several ancient cultures.[10] Pierre Hadot, who has perhaps done more than any contemporary scholar to retrieve and articulate this classical vision of philosophy, argues that contemporary philosophers have largely lost touch with this rich and varied heritage. As Hadot notes, for the ancient Greeks in particular philosophy involves much more than discourse and aims at being a comprehensive and distinct way of being-in-the-world that "engages the whole of existence."[11] The point of living a philosophical life from this ancient perspective is to make spiritual progress and to become a different—and, ultimately, better—person. The practice of philosophy thus involves and is intended to engender a conversion in us that "turns our entire life upside down."[12] Hadot suggests all ancient Greek schools (such as the Stoics, Epicureans, and Cynics) assume that, prior to the conversion to a philosophical way of life, human beings live inauthentically in "a state of unhappy disquiet," "consumed by worries, [and] torn by passions."[13] Philosophy's calling in this ancient context was to help deliver people from the anxieties and dissatisfactions of inauthenticity and to learn to live worthwhile, authentic lives (to use the language of the existentialists). Hadot is perhaps best known for his idea that this conversion to and constitution of a more authentic life was accomplished in the ancient context through different kinds of intellectual and physical practices—what he calls *spiritual exercises*. These exercises, which took different forms in different schools, all assume as their goal "training people to live and to look at the world in a new way."[14] Redirected away from our restless striving after the trivial "goods" of the dominant culture (egoism, luxury, wealth, social reputation, etc.), philosophy affords us the opportunity to look at the world with fresh eyes and determine anew how our lives should be directed. In this way, philosophy as a way of life is intended to help us see the world as if for the

---

10 See Michael Chase, Stephen R. L. Clark, and Michael McGhee, eds., *Philosophy as a Way of Life: Ancients and Moderns: Essays in Honor of Pierre Hadot* (Malden, MA: Wiley Blackwell, 2013), and James M. Ambury, Tushar Irani, and Kathleen Wallace, eds., *Philosophy as a Way of Life: Historical, Contemporary, and Pedagogical Perspectives* (Malden, MA: Wiley, 2021).
11 Pierre Hadot, *Philosophy as a Way of Life: Spiritual Exercises from Socrates to Foucault*, trans. Michael Chase (Malden, MA: Blackwell, 1995), 83.
12 Hadot, *Philosophy as a Way of Life*, 83.
13 Hadot, *Philosophy as a Way of Life*, 102.
14 Hadot, *Philosophy as a Way of Life*, 107.

first time and for the last time, and to build a way of life that befits this intense vision and focused disposition.

One of my goals in this book is to demonstrate that Jeffers's poetry seeks to enact something very much like this philosophical conversion in thought and life through his poetry. To be sure, his work does *not* aim to present that vision in the carefully organized and systematized way characteristic of ancient philosophical schools like the Stoics or Epicureans. But what Jeffers does offer is a new and compelling philosophical vision of the world—of the planet and the cosmos as a whole—and our place in it.[15] This vision, which is profoundly at odds with the anthropocentrism that dominates the history of the West from the ancients to the present, aims both to re-describe the general human condition and to reorient our concerns and loves in new ways beyond a narrowly interhuman register.

That it is necessary for us today to develop a fresh vision of the world and ourselves is one indication that practicing philosophy as a way of life is not simply a matter of uncritically retrieving the frameworks of ancient schools and traditions. Hadot emphasizes this point repeatedly in his own work, suggesting that the ontological views of the ancients are in many ways no longer tenable today and that the social contexts in which their specific practices were developed are fundamentally different from our own.[16] My aim, then, will not be to show how Jeffers's poetic vision can be reduced to, say, Platonism, Stoicism, Epicureanism, or Cynicism, despite Jeffers's inclination toward such themes as permanency, endurance, naturalism, and his affinity for the more-than-human world. Rather, I will suggest that the practice of philosophy today requires new ways of understanding ourselves and the world and new practices that help to reorient our daily lives. In crucial ways, Jeffers was a forerunner on the path of non-anthropocentric thinking and living, and I hope to demonstrate the ongoing relevance of his poetry and life for those of us who seek to take up such a path today.

Early Life and Conversion

Robinson Jeffers was born John Robinson Jeffers on January 10, 1887, in Allegheny, Pennsylvania, a city in the southwest portion of the state near

---

15 Jeffers himself characterizes his work as being philosophical in terms of its content and implications. See, for example, his remarks about the "philosophical attitude" (CP 4, 428) he endeavors to present throughout much of his work.

16 Hadot, *Philosophy as a Way of Life*, 273; see also Pierre Hadot, *The Present Alone Is Our Happiness: Conversations with Jeannie Carlier and Arnold I. Davidson*, 2nd. ed., trans. Marc Djaballah and Michael Chase (Stanford: Stanford University Press, 2011), 102–3.

the Ohio River (the city was later incorporated into the city of Pittsburgh).[17] The parents who welcomed Jeffers into the world, William Hamilton Jeffers and Annie Tuttle Jeffers, were separated in age by 22 years—a fact that created no little consternation among Annie's family when William proposed marriage. William was ordained as a Presbyterian minister and taught as a seminary professor. He specialized in languages and had facility with several, including Greek, Latin, Hebrew, and Aramaic. Before his marriage to Annie, William was married to a woman named Maria who came from a wealthy family; they had two children together, both of whom died at a young age. Maria herself died after she and William had been married only a brief time, leaving William a substantial inheritance from her estate. After the death of his first wife, and while guest pastoring at a church in Sewickley, William met and was enchanted by Annie, who had extensive training as a musician and played the organ for the church. Despite the differences in their ages, William proposed marriage to Annie, a proposal that she accepted with enthusiasm. The two were married in 1885, and Jeffers was born to Annie less than two years later.

William, the "grim clergyman" (to borrow Jeffers's description of his father [CP 3: 442]), valued his scholarship and seclusion above all else, which led to him constantly moving the Jeffers family from place to place to secure ideal working and living conditions. Within the first three years of Jeffers's life, William moved the family from Allegheny to nearby Sewickley and then to Edgeworth. The restless father also brought his family with him on frequent trips to Europe and enrolled Jeffers in kindergarten there, first in Zurich and the following year in Lucerne. When back home in Pennsylvania, William placed Jeffers in a variety of private schools and supplemented Jeffers's education at home, first by teaching him Greek and then Latin (literally slapping linguistic proficiency into Jeffers, as he recalls [CL 3, 795]). Unhappy with the results of Jeffers's schooling at home in the United States, William decided to enroll 11-year-old Robinson full time in European schools. From ages eleven to fifteen, Jeffers moved from one school to the next, with William never seeming quite satisfied with the institution he had chosen or the results produced. Jeffers attended a series of schools in Switzerland, Germany, and France, where the teaching was conducted entirely in foreign languages;

---

[17] The biographical details in this section are drawn from the following sources: Melba Berry Bennett, *The Stone Mason of Tor House: The Life and Works of Robinson Jeffers* (Los Angeles: The Ward Ritchie Press, 1966); James Karman, *Robinson Jeffers: Poet of California*, rev. ed. (Brownsville, OR: Story Line Press, 1995); and James Karman, *Robinson Jeffers: Poet and Prophet* (Stanford: Stanford University Press, 2015).

during this time, he became fluent in French and German while deepening his knowledge of Greek and Latin. Annie stayed with Jeffers (and Jeffers's brother, Hamilton, who was six years younger) in Europe while he was in school, and William traveled to Europe to visit while on break from his teaching duties.

Although Jeffers was not always pleased with the educational institutions in which he found himself, he flourished both physically and intellectually during this time. His classmates at Vevey nicknamed him "the little Spartan" because of his ability to tolerate swimming in icy cold water and for his courage in undertaking long, rigorous hikes in the mountains. Toward the end of his European schooling, Jeffers began to show a sustained interest in poetry and made some of his first efforts at writing his own verse. William, aware of this development, brought his 14-year-old son two volumes of poetry during one of his routine visits to Europe: one by Thomas Campbell and the other by Dante Gabriel Rossetti. Jeffers quickly set aside the Campbell volume but was utterly enraptured by Rossetti's poems.

> My first deeply felt encounter with poetry interests me; for it was rather bizarre, besides being one of the greatest pleasures I ever experienced. […] [No] lines of print will ever intoxicate me as Rossetti's rather florid verses did, from "The Blessed Damozel" to the least last sonnet. […] My pleasure was pure; I was never a critical reader, and was not yet looking for someone to imitate. And now, if I should ever wonder about the uses of poetry, I have only to remember that year's experience. (CP 4, 382–83)

When Jeffers was fifteen, William decided that his son's education in Europe was complete and that he should return to the United States for college. Jeffers was initially enrolled in a college in Pittsburgh before the family relocated (for reasons of William's health) to California, where Jeffers entered Occidental College. Jeffers's curriculum continued the language-based and humanities-based education he had undertaken in Europe and included such courses as Biblical Literature and Greek as well as courses in the physical sciences. Jeffers performed well in his classes at Occidental, contributed to the poetry magazine, and graduated at the young age of eighteen. He enrolled thereafter for graduate studies at University of Southern California, where he focused on languages and literature before abandoning this course of study. After a short stint at the University of Zurich, Jeffers returned to the United States and took up a rather different intellectual path, translating medical papers from German into English for a family physician. This translating work piqued Jeffers's interest in medical science and led him to enroll in medical school at the University of Southern California, where he performed exceptionally well. He ultimately left medical school without a degree, however, and ended up trying out a forestry program in Oregon, which he also ended up abandoning without a degree.

During this period, Jeffers was clearly having trouble deciding on a life-course. Intellectually precocious and erudite though he was, he lacked the maturity and resolve to choose a path and ended up drifting through various projects and relationships.[18] It was also during this time that Jeffers first met his future wife, Una Call Kuster. Una, who had wide-ranging intellectual interests and was enrolled in the same Goethe seminar at University of Southern California as Jeffers, was married at the time to a high-profile lawyer, but she was less interested in playing the role of a traditional wife and more interested in pursuing her own intellectual interests and development. Over time, Jeffers's and Una's relationship turned from friendly to romantic. They tried to end their relationship multiple times, but their attraction to each other proved too powerful. Una and her husband eventually divorced, and she married Jeffers immediately thereafter. Una and Jeffers were to remain together as a couple, despite occasional periods of marital turbulence, until Una's death nearly four decades later.

Jeffers's marriage to Una (in 1913) and the birth of twin sons, Garth and Donnan (in 1916), sharpened his existential crisis. He had by this time resolved to be a full-time poet, but his first published volumes were (despite their technical proficiency and occasional flashes of brilliance) largely uninspired and imitative—and Jeffers knew it. Where at one time he was far ahead of his peers in terms of intellectual sophistication and educational achievements, due to his long periods of drifting and writing second-rate poetry, he was now being eclipsed by the poets he held most in esteem. Jeffers was at a crossroads.

Just before the arrival of their twin sons, and in the midst of personal turmoil that included the loss of a baby daughter who lived only one day and the death of Jeffers's father William, Jeffers and Una moved to Carmel in northern California. After living in a cabin for a brief span, Jeffers decided to have a stone house built and apprenticed himself to the stone mason he hired. Jeffers became a competent mason in the process and began building his own stone structures in the form of additions to the house as well as a tower. (These structures, known as Tor House and Hawk Tower, remain standing to the present day and welcome numerous visitors each year.) Soon, a daily rhythm took shape for Jeffers: writing early in the morning, working

---

18 Jeffers's own appraisal of himself during this period is less generous: "not knowing what else to do [...] [I] drifted into mere drunken idleness" (CL 3, 795).

on stonemasonry and other projects (such as planting and tending trees) in the afternoon, spending time reading to the family in the evening, followed by late nights talking with Una and studying the stars. The family would also regularly take long hikes into the surrounding woods and hills on the weekends to explore the flora and fauna and share in the rugged beauty of the California coastline. Living in this rhythmic and deliberate manner, Jeffers underwent something like a subjective conversion. Una describes it in a letter as "a kind of awakening such as adolescents and religious converts are said to experience" (CL 2, 310).[19] While the precise nature of this conversion isn't spelled out in detail in the letter, the experience would manifestly and radically change the form and content of his poetry going forward.

It took considerable time, though, for this transformation to bear fruit. It was only a full six years after his conversion that Jeffers was finally able to create poetry that rose to the level of the insights he had gained during this time. But it didn't take long for critics to recognize the depth and force of his vision or the poetic mastery that marks these more mature poems. Beginning in the mid-1920s, Jeffers's work came to the attention of a number of prominent poets and literary critics (among them, George Sterling, James Rorty, Mark van Doren, and Babette Deutsch) who championed his work and helped it reach a wider public. At this time, Jeffers's self-published volume of poetry, *Tamar* (1924), was acquired by Boni and Liveright and expanded and re-published as *Roan Stallion, Tamar and Other Poems* in 1925. The work sold well, received multiple laudatory reviews, and established virtually overnight Jeffers's reputation as one of the leading American poets of his era.

Jeffers's life from this point forward is often told from the perspective of his long string of publications (some dozen volumes of poetry with major publishers), his rise to fame (gracing the cover of *Time* magazine in 1932, having his adaptation of Medea performed on Broadway to critical acclaim in 1947), and his gradual decline into obscurity (at least among the bulk of professional literary critics, but not general readers). These sorts of biographical details are not my primary concern in this study, though I will touch on certain biographical points of interest where relevant in the chapters that follow. What is of primary interest for our purposes is trying to make sense of the vision that Jeffers arrives at in his early-to-mid-30s, a vision that animates all of his mature poetry. What insights did Jeffers gain in his daily work with stone, in his day-to-day life on the edge of the Pacific Ocean, and in his regular walks and excursions into the Santa Lucia mountains? What did he see and

---

19 Una's words here are actually a direct quotation from notes prepared by Jeffers himself (see CL 2, 311).

encounter that could have inspired such prodigious and passionate poetry for such a sustained period of time? What occasioned this "accidental new birth" (CL 2, 1049) of Jeffers's mind? What events going on in the world around him—political, economic, social, ecological—convinced Jeffers that it was necessary to direct his poetic attention increasingly toward the more-than-human world? It is to these questions that I turn in the following pages.[20]

Inhumanism

If we were to give a single name to the vision that animates Jeffers's mature poetry, we could hardly do better than *inhumanism*. Jeffers himself uses this term to describe his work, most notably in the Preface to the collection of controversial poems that form one of his late books, *The Double Axe* (1948). Yet, despite the aptness of the term *inhumanism* for capturing Jeffers's concerns, its use today could lead to confusion given other uses of the term currently in circulation. The concept of inhumanism has recently come into vogue in theoretical and critical circles; and some of the senses the term carries there are rather different from those that characterize Jeffers's project. So, before explaining more fully what Jeffers means by inhumanism, we should first gain a sense of how and why this concept is being used today, and then see how Jeffers's work both anticipates and challenges key aspects of this trend.

For those who work in the humanities and social sciences today, the question of how to think about "the human" has become a leading concern. The question is crucial for these fields, given that they are grounded on what is sometimes called an *anthropological difference*—that is, a difference that distinguishes human beings from other beings, both natural and artificial. Although it might seem a self-evident fact, it is worth reminding ourselves that the humanities are focused on the study of *human* languages, literatures, arts and so on, while the social sciences focus on various registers (economic, political, etc.) of *human* society—which means that the work carried out in these fields, which often comprises roughly half of the research done in contemporary universities, is grounded on a series of fundamental decisions about who or what is human and how human beings are essentially different from other sorts of beings. But it is precisely this claim to an anthropological difference, to a human distinctive, that is currently being called fundamentally

---

20 For readers who desire a fuller account of the details of Jeffers's biography and how his life can be fitted together with the narrative arc of his work, I recommend Karman, *Robinson Jeffers: Poet and Prophet*. I am thankful to an anonymous reviewer for calling my attention to the importance of this issue.

into question. Not only is it being increasingly acknowledged that human social and intellectual developments cannot be understood without accounting for human relations with the more-than-human world (animals, plants, and various organic and inorganic systems), but it is not at all clear that trying to discern an anthropological difference (or set of anthropological differences) is still a tenable or worthwhile project. Advances in biology that have undercut claims to essential distinctions between human beings and animals (and other life forms), coupled with developments in artificial intelligence, genetics, and related fields, have raised fresh and pressing questions about whether there really is something that makes human beings distinct among the field of beings that populate the planet.

The intellectual, material, and socio-critical challenges to traditional notions of the human have led to a bewildering variety of substitutes and alternatives in recent years. From the multiple iterations of anti-humanism among mid-century poststructuralist philosophers, to the post-humanisms and transhumanisms that erupted in the late twentieth century and that have continued to multiply into the present, there has been no shortage of attempts to move "beyond the human" in one way or another. Among these alternatives to humanism, a trend has developed during this period that employs the conceptual vocabulary of inhumanism.[21] One of the most influential analyses of inhumanism is found in the work of Jean-François Lyotard (who is also largely responsible for the wide usage of the term *postmodernism*, another theme that is intimately related to the critique of humanism). In contrast to Jeffers, Lyotard is less interested in endorsing the notion of the inhuman and more interested in exhorting readers to beware of the effects of living in an era that he believes is becoming more and more inhuman. In a collection of essays published in 1988, Lyotard famously anticipates developments in artificial intelligence that threaten to render certain human distinctives obsolete (concerns that might have seemed overstated at the time but appear

---

21 My survey of the concept of inhumanism aims chiefly to highlight uses of the term that are relevant to my analysis of Jeffers's work. For a more comprehensive survey of the contemporary terrain, see Julian Murphet, "A Modest Proposal for the Inhuman," *Modernism/modernity* 23 (2016): 651–70. I should also note that I retain the term *inhumanism* despite sharing many of the same reservations that Julietta Singh raises concerning the way this concept tends today to lose track "in its own grammatical formulation of the histories, practices, and narratives that make some human and cast others outside its orbit" (Julietta Singh, *Unthinking Mastery: Dehumanism and Decolonial Entanglements* [Durham: Duke University Press, 2017], 5). I hope the pages that follow, as well as other work I have written on the question of the human, make clear my commitment to contesting, and to articulating alternatives to, this uneven distribution of humanity.

rather matter-of-fact today).[22] Not only does Lyotard believe we are becoming increasingly like machines in various ways (e.g., through the widespread use of artificial prostheses and implants, and due to having to live and work in conditions that force us to function like automata), we are also at risk of being replaced by machines—at least if the ruling class realizes its dreams of full automation. Despite Lyotard's close association with political radicalism, he adopts (and with some irony, to be sure) a strikingly conservative and humanist attitude toward these trends in late modernity. Against the capitalist-techno-science complex and the inhumanity of its system, Lyotard advocates maintaining our non-machine-like humanity and resisting the blurring of boundaries between human beings and machines. For Lyotard, then, even though our present condition and immediate future can rightly be described as inhumanist, it is a condition he believes we should resist in the name of maintaining and experimenting with the rich variety of human potentials and possibilities that open up plural worlds and differing ways of life.

More celebratory concepts of inhumanism were taking form around this time as well, many of them inspired by Donna Haraway's "A Manifesto for Cyborgs."[23] Haraway makes the case in this essay that the leaky boundaries between human beings and various others (machine, animal, etc.) are to be affirmed as sites for experiments in becoming something other-than-human rather than as threats to any proper humanity we might believe we possess. Here, the inhuman takes the form of various monstrosities and sublime figures that exceed our cognitive mastery and with which we have to reckon anew in light of our post-theological present and the loss of traditional religious coordinates. More recent explorations of this aspect of the inhumanist terrain are found in thinkers like Reza Negarestani and Ray Brassier, who (like Lyotard) have no interest in utterly abolishing or further humiliating the human but seek instead (and rather differently from Lyotard) to explore the inhuman consequences of human reason when pushed to its own limits.[24] For thinkers inspired by this more "speculative" aspect of the inhuman, the human mind itself contains tendencies and capacities that are fundamentally alien and inhuman ("human" here being understood in terms of traditional

---

22 Jean-François Lyotard, *The Inhuman: Reflections on Time*, trans. Geoffrey Bennington and Rachel Bowlby (Stanford: Stanford University Press, 1991).
23 Donna J. Haraway, "A Manifesto for Cyborgs: Science, Technology, and Socialist Feminism in the 1980s," *Socialist Review* 15 (1985): 65–107.
24 See Reza Negarestani, "The Labor of the Inhuman," in *#ACCELERATE#*, ed. Robin Mackay and Armen Avanessian (Falmouth, UK: Urbanomic, 2014), 425–66; and Ray Brassier, "Prometheanism and its Critics," in *#ACCELERATE#*, ed. Robin Mackay and Armen Avanessian (Falmouth, UK: Urbanomic, 2014), 467–88.

conceptions of human nature, subjectivity, consciousness, etc.). What is more, this approach suggests that inhuman tendencies carry with them the potential to transform fundamentally what we understand by the human condition, inasmuch as inhuman potentials emerge from, interact with, and ultimately open up new evolutionary paths for human existence.

While both of these approaches to inhumanism (i.e., the critical Lyotardian approach and the more affirmative speculative approach just mentioned) have certain parallels in Jeffers's thought (parallels I touch on at various points in the following chapters), they are not the primary valences he attaches to the term. Closer to the core of Jeffers's concerns is the notion of inhumanism developed by another influential contemporary theorist, Elizabeth Grosz, whose work makes use of themes from the writings of Charles Darwin, Gilles Deleuze, and others to rethink the distinction between the human and the inhuman.[25] For Grosz, rather than taking the human as the starting point and viewing the inhuman as its antithesis, inhuman existence should be understood as being more fundamental than the human and as something both internal and external to human existence. In particular, Grosz suggests we should understand the earth and the cosmos more generally as populated by a range of unruly pre-individual and impersonal forces (her primary figures for the inhuman) that can neither be brought fully within the boundaries of human society nor domesticated by our modes of thought and technology. Yet, the status of inhuman existence as being something more fundamental than and outside the human and its thought and institutions does not, for all that, leave the human and inhuman in utterly separate spheres. Instead, Grosz locates the inhuman at the very heart of human existence and argues that it serves as the condition of possibility for human life: human beings emerge in, through, and from the inhuman forces, energies, and relations that populate the earth and cosmos. Further, the inhuman stands as an ongoing principle of interruption in human culture and society that prods human beings to respond, invent, and form new ways of living.[26]

Although Jeffers employs a somewhat different vocabulary and set of theoretical concepts to articulate his notion of inhumanism, with Grosz's

---

25 See Elizabeth Grosz, *Chaos, Territory, Art: Deleuze and the Framing of the Earth* (New York: Columbia University Press, 2008); and Elizabeth Grosz, *The Incorporeal: Ontology, Ethics, and the Limits of Materialism* (New York: Columbia University Press, 2017).

26 A prime example of such a relation is how the earth and planetary cycles are now seen as actors in their own right in relation to climate change and other forms of ecological degradation, inhuman agents that pressure and provoke us to rethink our collective way of life from the ground up. On this notion, see Bruno Latour, *Down to Earth: Politics in the New Climatic Regime*, trans. Catherine Porter (Medford, MA: Polity, 2018).

approach we have arrived on terrain closely related to that which Jeffers occupies. As with Grosz, Jeffers's notion of inhumanism is meant to emphasize the existence of something "outside" the boundaries of human culture and society, an outside that precedes human evolution, that continues as a force of interruption and creativity in the present, and that will outlast us as human individuals and as a species. Jeffers maintains that part of becoming mature as human individuals and as a species is recognizing this outside and affirming our position and existence relative to it. At the same time, he goes well beyond Grosz in making a number of rather bold claims about the appropriate normative posture to adopt to the inhuman realities that exceed us. For Jeffers, our lives can be rendered meaningful and worthwhile only if we learn to *love* inhuman realities (and not just acknowledge and affirm them as Grosz would have it). He maintains that it is the inhuman world, and our ability to find ourselves anew in and among that world, that allows us to live—and live well—in the midst of the difficulties of existence (a theme I will discuss at more length in Chapter 1). Without this affective, passionate disposition toward inhuman existence animating our lives, Jeffers believes we will all-too-easily fall prey to pessimism and come to believe that life is ultimately not worth the effort. The task of Jeffers's poetry, then, is to sketch a way of thinking and living that encourages a passionate affirmation of the more-than-human world and that, in turn, allows us to be "born again," or reconstituted, as inhuman subjects.

A Guide for Readers

My reading of Jeffers begins in Chapter 1 with his well-known poem "Apology for Bad Dreams." This rich and complex piece raises the issue of what I refer to as *the "other" problem of evil*, which is to say, the problem of evil that arises for those who live and think from a this-worldly, immanent perspective. This problem is particularly acute for a poet like Jeffers who seeks to affirm the value and beauty of the world, even in the face of its evident violence and cruelty and without having recourse to a supernatural entity to explain or justify the presence of such evils (as is the case with the classical theological version of the problem of evil). While Jeffers's poetry often recalls us to the disturbing examples of evil characteristic of modern wars, mass culture, and industrialized society (a theme he shares with many of his contemporaries), he does not limit his analysis of violence and cruelty to the interhuman register. Instead, he views evil and useless suffering as inhering in the very fabric of existence and extending well beyond the orbit of human beings. Thus, if we are to affirm the value and beauty of existence in the face of its manifold and manifest difficulties, he believes we need a different and richer understanding of the nature of things and an alternative picture of how the whole of things hangs together. The following chapters sketch in the contours of that picture.

In Chapter 2, I examine Jeffers's critical attitude toward the religious and political saviors who promise to deliver human beings from the evils and difficulties of existence. Much like his near contemporary Sigmund Freud, Jeffers believes that civilized life and its religious and political structures create as many problems as they solve. But whereas Freud thinks that the best chance for increased human happiness comes from trying to reform civilization in a post-religious direction, Jeffers believes Western civilization has entered a period of decline from which it will not exit and, hence, that reform is a bankrupt project. While Jeffers's critical analysis of civilization would seem to logically indicate a turn toward individualist anarchism, I suggest that his work articulates an altogether different orientation, one in which human beings might turn instead to the inhuman beauty of things as a ground from which to re-orient and re-anchor their individual and collective ways of life.

Chapter 3 elaborates on some of the foundational elements of what is involved in making that turn, with particular focus on the cosmic and onto-epistemological[27] aspects of the inhumanist perspective. Jeffers had a front-row seat to a number of important advances in astronomy that occurred during his lifetime, and he aims to bring those findings to bear on the status of the human condition and on the meaning of our everyday lives. I suggest that the cosmic perspective adopted by Jeffers serves on the one hand to further decenter human beings in the larger scope of things while at the same time intensifying appreciation for the myriad wonders of daily, earthly life. The chapter closes with a discussion of Jeffers's reflections on truth, a notion which for him involves attending to the ways in which the wonders and beauty of the inhuman world interrupt our standard ways of life and grace us with access to another world behind our everyday world.

Chapter 4 turns to Jeffers's critical analysis of human nature and traditional notions of humanism. The chapter begins with a reading of Jeffers's narrative "The Humanist's Tragedy," in which he revisits and reworks central themes and scenes in Euripides's *The Bacchae*. Here Jeffers explores the various dimensions of the humanist project that must be overcome on the path toward inhumanism. Jeffers's works in this vein have often led to him being labeled a misanthrope and pessimist. I argue instead that his critique of the human is intended to open the space for experiments in becoming something other-than-human, not in the sense of changing biological species

---

27 Ontological refers to the study of the most basic nature of reality, while epistemology has to do with theories of knowledge acquisition.

but in the sense of a fundamental reordering of one's subjectivity away from all-too-human affairs and interests.

Continuing the themes introduced in the previous chapter, Chapter 5 examines in more detail the alternative values that correspond to an inhumanist reorientation. I look at the recurring problem that Jeffers's protagonists seem to have with breaking "the mold" of humanity and what sorts of practices and perspectives make it possible to sustain such a break. I also examine how the inhumanist values and ideals championed by Jeffers might serve to reframe what is stake at the level of collective politics. In the Conclusion, I discuss Jeffers's Preface to *The Double Axe*, which contains a succinct statement of his inhumanist commitments, as a way of consolidating and summarizing the previous chapters. I also return to the other problem of evil with which the book begins in order to consider how the inhumanist perspective reframes the issue of evil and opens the path to an affirmative, post-anthropocentric way of life.

Chapter 1

EVIL

Jeffers's "Apology for Bad Dreams" (CP 1, 208–11; SP, 141–44), one of his most frequently cited and analyzed poems, opens with a forceful and memorable description of the beauty of the California coast.[1]

> In the purple light, heavy with redwood, the slopes drop seaward,
> Headlong convexities of forest, drawn in together to the steep ravine.
>   Below, on the sea-cliff,
> A lonely clearing; a little field of corn by the streamside; a roof under
>   spared trees. Then the ocean
> Like a great stone someone has cut to a sharp edge and polished to
>   shining. Beyond it, the fountain
> And furnace of incredible light flowing up from the sunk sun. (CP 1,
>   208; SP, 141)

What initially appears to be a straightforwardly loco-descriptive poem shifts dramatically in its sixth line to an account of a disturbing event unfolding on the clearing below: a woman is punishing and beating a horse.

> She had tied the halter to a sapling at the edge of the wood, but when
>   the great whip
> Clung to the flanks the creature kicked so hard she feared he would
>   snap the halter; she called from the house

---

[1] Helpful readings of this piece include: Robert J. Brophy, *Robinson Jeffers: Myth, Ritual, and Symbol in his Narrative Poems* (Cleveland: Case Western Reserve University Press, 1973), 255–83; Robert J. Brophy, "Jeffers's 'Apology for Bad Dreams' Revisited," *Jeffers Studies* 8, no. 2 (2004): 3–19; Tim Hunt, "A Poetics of Witness: Jeffers's 'Salmon Fishing' and the Apology in 'Apology for Bad Dreams,'" *Jeffers Studies* 10.2–11.2 (2009): 1–17; and Robert Zaller, *Robinson Jeffers and the American Sublime* (Stanford: Stanford University Press, 2012), 189–99.

> The young man her son, who fetched a chain tie-rope, they working together
> Noosed the small rusty links round the horse's tongue
> And tied him by the swollen tongue to the tree.
> Seen from this height they are shrunk to insect size.
> Out of all human relation. You cannot distinguish
> The blood dripping from where the chain is fastened,
> The beast shuddering […]
> You cannot see the face of the woman. (CP 1, 208; SP, 141)

Immediately after depicting this painful scene at a distance, the narrator returns to a description of the natural backdrop against which the horse beating unfolds:

> The enormous light beats up out of the west across the cloud-bars of the trade-wind. The ocean
> Darkens, the high clouds brighten, the hills darken together. Unbridled and unbelievable beauty
> Covers the evening world […] not covers, grows apparent out of it, as Venus down there grows out
> From the lit sky. What said the prophet? "I create good: and I create evil: I am the Lord." (CP 1, 208–9; SP, 141–42)

This sort of staging of a stark contrast between the supreme beauties of the world and its heartbreaking cruelties is ubiquitous in Jeffers's poetry; and the question of how to make sense of this opposition is, in many ways, the central issue animating his work. Does the senseless cruelty described here—the violent noosing and beating of a horse—overwhelm and cancel out the beauty of the surrounding landscape? Do the opposing aspects of reality belong to or necessitate one another in some sense? Is there a larger frame that might help to explain how such terrible cruelty and such tremendous beauty can exist side by side? Further, is this complex and seemingly contradictory reality something ultimately to be affirmed or rejected?

The "Other" Problem of Evil

Raised in a deeply religious household, Jeffers was as a youth in regular contact with the words of the Hebrew prophets (as the variation on Isaiah 45:7 in the lines cited above would indicate) and Christian confessional texts. Through that exposure, he certainly would have been familiar with the problem of evil as it arises in a Christian context. The Church Father Augustine's classical formulation of this problem identifies the "sore point" concerning evil for Christian believers: "Now we believe that everything that exists comes from the one God, although God is not the author of sins. But this is the sore point: If sins come from the souls that God created, and those souls come from God, how is it that sins are not almost immediately traced back to God?"[2] The subsequent Christian tradition has offered dozens of ways of "solving" this problem, all of which seek to render God just and find some way to absolve Him from being responsible for evil in the world, both anthropogenic and natural.

Whether such theodicies are logically persuasive is a question I set aside here. What is important to note for our purposes is that this traditional Christian way of understanding and dealing with the world's evils gradually became untenable for Jeffers as he matured to adulthood; and his advanced studies in modern science and medicine as a graduate student only served to reinforce a skepticism about Christianity that had begun to emerge in the years prior. Reverend Dr. Barclay, the main protagonist of Jeffers's early epic poem, *The Women at Point Sur* (1927), provides a succinct statement on the epistemological status of Christian beliefs in contemporary times. Speaking to his parishioners during a Sunday morning service, Barclay confesses:

> I have nothing true to tell you, no profession but ignorance. I can tell you what's false. Christianity is false.
> The fable that Christ was the son of God and died to save you, died and lived again. Lies. (CP 1, 250)

Although Jeffers's person is not to be conflated with that of his fictional character Barclay, this statement surely reflects his own mature conclusions about the falseness of Christianity and the impossibility for him in subscribing to its dogmas or adopting its liturgies and practices.

But the loss of faith in his childhood Christianity did not, for Jeffers, signal a simple victory for a disenchanted atheism. There is in Jeffers none of the smug triumphalism that we find in the discourse of today's new atheists, no mocking of religious beliefs or of the passion for living a worthwhile life. Further, we find in Jeffers's work a keen sense that the problem of evil functions not simply as a defeater of traditional religious beliefs but instead poses a fundamental, perhaps *the* fundamental, challenge to a life lived entirely

---

2 Augustine, *On the Free Choice of the Will, On Grace and Free Choice, and Other Writings*, ed. and trans. Peter King (New York: Cambridge University Press, 2010), 5.

within a naturalistic, "immanent frame."[3] In other words, Jeffers's *oeuvre* is built on the lucid acknowledgment that the evils of the world do not simply disappear if one moves beyond belief in the supernatural and a traditionally religious worldview and way of life; rather, they persist and must be dealt with anew, lest these evils cast doubt on the value of existence as such. For looking squarely at the difficulties of life without any explanation or consolation threatens to usher in the most acidic forms of nihilism and pessimism—a consequence that, to be sure, plagued Jeffers's poetry from beginning to end but that he almost always sought to contest and repel.[4]

Acknowledging that the evils of the world must be accounted for and explained anew if one inhabits an immanent frame is what I will call the "other" problem of evil. This problem arises for anyone who adheres to what Nietzsche labels "honest atheism"[5] and who pursues the affirmative task of trying to articulate what form a worthwhile life might take given that starting point. The other problem of evil also involves what we could describe as a sea change in the very nature of what is called evil, a shift that occurred squarely in the midst of Jeffers's career as a poet. Born in the 1880s, Jeffers grew up in and lived through a host of tumultuous world-historical events: the rise of fascism and totalitarianism, two World Wars, technological revolutions and mass-industrialization, a global economic depression, colonial genocide, and the Holocaust, to name but a handful. These events brought with them untold violence and countless deaths—suffering on a scale unimaginable by previous generations. For Jeffers and other intellectuals of his generation, this change in the very nature of evil called for both a novel account and response.

The Jewish philosopher Emmanuel Levinas, who lost his entire birth family in the Holocaust, attests poignantly to the change in the form and nature of evil that occurs during this time. As Levinas explains:

---

3 This concept is developed by Charles Taylor in his *A Secular Age* (Cambridge, MA: Harvard University Press, 2007). Taylor briefly engages Jeffers's poetry in this work (665–67).

4 In response to the suggestion from a correspondent that he was a pessimist, Jeffers responded: "as to 'pessimist'; that should mean believing in the worst—that things are as bad as possible. I can imagine them a great deal worse. Things are as they are; and the world is full of wretchedness yet very beautiful. And not all wretched" (CL 2, 440).

5 Friedrich Nietzsche, *The Gay Science: With a Prelude in Rhymes and an Appendix of Songs*, trans. Walter Kaufmann (New York: Vintage Books, 1974), 307. Nietzsche uses this phrase to describe Arthur Schopenhauer's atheism, but he contests the pessimistic consequences Schopenhauer draws from such atheism. Whether Jeffers himself can be accurately described simply or only as an atheist is a question that I return to in subsequent chapters.

This is the century that in thirty years has known two world wars, the totalitarianism of right and left, Hitlerism and Stalinism, Hiroshima, the Gulag, and the genocides of Auschwitz and Cambodia. This is the century which is drawing to a close in the haunting memory of the return of everything signified by these barbaric names: suffering and evil are deliberately imposed, yet no reason sets limits to the exasperation of a reason become political and detached from all ethics.

Among these events the Holocaust of the Jewish people under the reign of Hitler seems to us the paradigm of gratuitous human suffering, where evil appears in its diabolical horror. This is perhaps not a subjective feeling. The disproportion between suffering and every theodicy was shown at Auschwitz with a glaring, obvious clarity. Its possibility puts into question the multi-millennial traditional faith. Did not the word of Nietzsche on the death of God take on, in the extermination camps, the signification of a quasi-empirical fact?[6]

For Levinas, who remained a practicing Jew throughout his life, evils of the sort named here cannot be justified using traditional theodicies such as those found in mainstream Judeo-Christian philosophy and theology. Traditional theodicies, which try to explain (or explain away) the evils of the world, reach a limit in the face of radical evil. To suggest that the classical notion of God (as omnipotent, omniscient, omnipresent, etc.) can be somehow squared with such evil is, Levinas argues, not only a childish task but an indecent one. Rather than trying to justify or explain evil with the consolations of a theodicy, Levinas instead maintains that we are called to respond to and resist the evils of the world by sustaining and deepening the inter-human ethical order established by ancient faith traditions.[7] This inter-human order contests the evils of the world by way of both rituals of attention that recall us to the vulnerability of other persons as well as through the adoption of concrete practices in our daily lives that move us in the direction of social justice. There is, for Levinas, no transcendent God to ensure that such an order is upheld; only our own distinctively human efforts and vigilance can limit the evils of the world and give rise to individual and collective ways of life that render existence more just and more worthwhile.

---

6 Emmanuel Levinas, "Useless Suffering," in *The Provocation of Levinas: Rethinking the Other*, ed. Robert Bernasconi and David Wood (London: Routledge, 1988), 156–67, citation at 161–62.
7 Levinas, "Useless Suffering," 164–65.

The Evil of the Sword

Levinas here presents us with something like a demythologized account of ethics and religion, where the name of God is retained but is emptied of its traditional supernatural significance.[8] In many ways, Jeffers's poetry can be read as offering a parallel version of such a project, but one stemming from a post-Calvinist Christian orientation rather than from a Talmudic-Jewish one. Jeffers's work, too, proceeds under the assumption that the nature of evil has changed in modernity and that traditional religious responses to evil are inadequate for addressing this change. In contrast to Levinas, though, Jeffers's understanding of the scope of evil is much broader and brings within its orbit violence directed at the more-than-human world (as the horse beating scene from "Apology" suggests). Likewise, Jeffers's response to evil is more varied in scope than Levinas's in terms of the relations at stake and what constitutes alternative values and ideals. Put simply, Jeffers does not limit the other problem of evil strictly to examining interhuman forms of evil and articulating fitting interhuman responses; instead, he sees the problem of evil as involving the more-than-human world and believes that an appropriate response to this problem involves reconstituting relations with both human and more-than-human others. Indeed, if we follow Jeffers's path of thought, we will ultimately be led to *reverse* this lexical ordering of relational reconstitution, placing the emphasis on rethinking and reworking relations with the more-than-human and inhuman world and allotting interhuman affairs a lesser but proportionally fitting attention.

Let's examine in more detail, then, Jeffers's understanding of evil and the particular forms it takes in contemporary times. Similar to the other great poets of his era who serve as the "antennae of the race,"[9] Jeffers cannot help but be struck by the miseries that attend life in industrialized cities. He makes special and recurrent note of the senseless suffering of modern existence, referring to the countless countries "clotted with human anguish" (CP 2, 415), "the storm of the sick nations, the rage of the hunger-smitten cities" (CP 1, 6; SP, 19), and the violence of everyday life evident in the "squalid savagery," "mass war" and "other evils / That make humanity ridiculous" (CP 2, 310;

---

8 For Levinas's remarks on demythologization, see Emmanuel Levinas, *Is It Righteous to Be? Interviews with Emmanuel Levinas*, ed. Jill Robbins (Stanford: Stanford University Press, 2001), 240–41.

9 Ezra Pound, *Literary Essays of Ezra Pound*, ed. T. S. Eliot (New York: New Directions, 1968), 297. Along these lines, Pound further suggests that "it is the business of the artist to make humanity aware of itself," a task that is certainly a key part of Jeffers's own poetic project.

SP, 399). These evils are deliberately inflicted by a war machine and perverse socioeconomic order that produces "unimaginable agonies […]. Not a few thousand but uncounted millions, not a day but years, pain, horror, sick hatred; / Famine that dries the children to little bones and huge eyes; high explosive that fountains dirt, flesh and bone-splinters" (CP 3, 124; SP, 581).

Modern humanity, Jeffers suggests, is characterized so pervasively by the return of the "age of tyrants" (CP 2, 558; SP, 541) and its "grand and fatal movements toward death," that "tearing pity / For the atoms of the mass, the persons, the victims" (CP 2, 515; SP, 513) is rendered vain. Such pity makes fools of those who desperately wish (no doubt like Jeffers himself) to fundamentally alter modern society's course: "I would burn my right hand in a slow fire / To change the future" (CP 2, 515; SP, 513). Jeffers had a personal stake, of course, in the kinds of evil he describes here—thus, the reference to burning one's hand in a slow fire constitutes something more than a throw-away line. He endured many a "night without sleep" (CP 2, 558–9) over the ongoing military violence; he also had two sons who were of military age during World War II and who could potentially be drafted and put directly in harm's way.[10]

In the vatic piece "Contemplation of the Sword"—written directly in the midst of the turmoil preceding World War II—Jeffers reflects on the global march to war, suggesting that "the sword" rather than reason will ultimately decide how this moment in history will unfold. He explains that "the sword" here refers not to the "obsolete instrument of bronze or steel used to kill men" but to the entire war apparatus:

> […] the storms and counterstorms of general destruction; killing of men,
> Destruction of all goods and materials; massacre, more or less intentional of children and women;
> Destruction poured down from wings, the air made accomplice, the innocent air
> Perverted into assassin and poisoner. (CP 2, 544; SP, 527)

The sword brings with it in its wake:

> […] weeping and despair, mass-enslavement, mass-torture, frustration of all hopes

---

10 One son, Garth, was in fact called to military duty and served as an army combat MP in Germany (Audry Lynch, *Garth Jeffers Recalls his Father, Robinson Jeffers: Recollections of a Poet's Son* [Lewiston, New York: Edwin Mellen Press, 2012], 48).

> That starred man's forehead. Tyranny for freedom, horror for happiness, famine for bread, carrion for children. (CP 2, 544; SP, 527)

Jeffers here writes personally and tenderly of his twin sons, born under the dark sky of World War I and now at risk for being drafted into World War II.

> I have two sons whom I love. They are twins, they were born in nineteen sixteen, which seemed to us a dark year
> Of a great war, and they are now of the age
> That war prefers. The first-born is like his mother, he is so beautiful
> That persons I hardly know have stopped me on the street to speak of the grave beauty of the boy's face.
> The second-born has strength for his beauty; when he strips for swimming the hero shoulders and wrestler loins
> Make him seem clothed. The sword: that is: loathsome disfigurements, blindness, mutilation, locked lips of boys
> Too proud to scream.
>
> Reason will not decide at last: the sword will decide. (CP 2, 545; SP, 528)

It is precisely these sorts of evils associated with modern war that make the other problem of evil so acute for a poet like Jeffers, who refuses all supernatural forms of justification or consolation. Typical forms of "evil," such as pain or death, Jeffers notes, can be dealt with, perhaps even affirmed ("I know what pain is, but pain can shine. I know what death is, I have sometimes / Longed for it" [CP 2, 544–45; SP, 527–8]). Such suffering can in some cases be used or useful, redeemed or redeemable. Ancient philosophical schools such as the Stoics, Cynics, and Epicureans built elaborate theoretical frameworks and ascetic disciplines to help practitioners deal with these forms of suffering and to incorporate them into a life that generally led toward flourishing; we find similar strategies for dealing with adversity among later philosophers such as Spinoza and Nietzsche, both of whom try to deal with evil in a naturalistic manner and avoid casting aspersions on existence because of its presence. But, as Jeffers emphasizes, the "cruelty and slavery and degradation, pestilence, filth, the pitifulness" (CP 2, 545; SP, 528) that characterize the modern age of the sword are things that cannot be so easily affirmed. These are examples of what Levinas rightly describes as "useless suffering," suffering that is utterly in vain and cannot be recuperated into any meaningful project. For a poet-philosopher like Jeffers, who desires to find beauty in the world and to affirm what life brings, such superfluous evils[11] can make it well-nigh impossible to praise the world "with a whole heart" (CP 2, 544; SP, 527).

Jeffers's reflections on evil are also sketched against the backdrop of the emergence and spread of a new form of society—namely, "mass society"—that, because of its ubiquitous, globalized nature, effectively undercuts the possibility of developing an alternative way of life. As with many writers and poets of his generation, Jeffers was sharply critical of the trends and moods of mass society; and he had little faith that there was much of anything worth preserving in this form of culture. In "The Broken Balance," he contrasts the lives of other animals (who "live their felt natures," who "understand life" and "live it to the brim") with those of the human beings of mass society who mold themselves "to the anthill" and who have "choked / Their natures until the souls die in them" (CP 1, 373; SP, 161). Having "sold themselves for toys and protection," they are an

> Uneasy and fractional people, having no center
> But in the eyes and mouths that surround them,
> Having no function but to serve and support
> Civilization, the enemy of man,
> No wonder they live insanely, and desire
> With their tongues, progress; with their eyes, pleasure; with their
>   hearts, death. (CP 1, 374; SP, 162)

Similarly, in "The Trap," Jeffers confesses his "alien" relation to mass society. The "toys: motors, music boxes, / Paper, fine clothes, leisure, diversion" and way of life associated with "the new abundance" and "other conveniences leave me cold" (CP 2, 415).

This civilizational apparatus functions, Jeffers suggests, in much the same way as a purse-seine surrounds and captures sardines in its netting. Like sardines, we modern inhabitants of mass society have also been circled by a skiff and the bottom of the net is now being pursed:

> [...] We have geared the machines and locked all together into interde-
>   pendence; we have built the great cities; now
> There is no escape. We have gathered vast populations incapable of
>   free survival, insulated

---

11 This is a term used by Adi Ophir in *The Order of Evils: Toward an Ontology of Morals*, trans. Rela Mazali and Havi Carel (New York: Zone Books, 2005).

> From the strong earth, each person in himself helpless, on all depend-
> ent. The circle is closed, and the net
> Is being hauled in. (CP 2, 518; SP, 515)

The simile suggests that we modern city dwellers are effectively trapped, hemmed in by the rhythms and routines of contemporary society, and that getting free will be all but impossible. But if a full escape from the structures of modern society is not possible, a change of location might be a live option—at least for those individuals with the economic means to undertake one. Mabel Dodge Luhan, a wealthy art patron who sought to rub elbows with famous writers and figures of the day, frequently invited Jeffers to her large desert home in New Mexico, a place that served for her and other elites as a sort of retreat from the hectic rhythms of life in mass society. Jeffers made the trek to New Mexico with his family several times (begrudgingly, for he preferred his daily way of life at Tor House), but those visits never produced the kind of poetic inspiration for Jeffers that Luhan hoped it would. Jeffers penned only one poem that spoke directly to his time there, a lyric entitled "New Mexican Mountain." This piece is unflinching in the critical eye it casts on settlers who try to escape the madness of mass society by leaving cities behind and appropriating traditional Indigenous cultures. Invited to watch a traditional corn dance ceremony put on for American tourists, Jeffers reflects:

> These tourists have eyes, the hundred watching the dance, white
>   Americans, hungrily too, with reverence, not laughter;
> Pilgrims from civilization, anxiously seeking beauty, religion, poetry;
>   pilgrims from the vacuum.
>
> People from cities, anxious to be human again. Poor show how they
>   suck you empty! The Indians are emptied,
> And certainly there was never religion enough, nor beauty nor poetry
>   here […] to fill Americans. (CP 2, 158; SP, 380)

Although Jeffers's work demonstrates considerable sensitivity to and sympathy with Indigenous cultures, he does not see this sort of inauthentic appropriation of those traditions as a solution to the problems and evils that plague modern-day civilizations.[12] The anxiety and restlessness that haunts the

---

12 For a brilliant discussion of Jeffers's complex relation to colonialism and the displacement of native American peoples, see Geneva Gano, *The Little Art Colony and US Modernism: Carmel, Provincetown, Taos* (Edinburgh: Edinburgh University Press, 2020).

tourist cannot be solved by trading one culture for another but must be confronted head on and dealt with on its own terms.

Natural Evil

> Who hears the fishes when they cry?
>
> —*Henry David Thoreau*[13]

Just as Jeffers maintains that it is essential to develop an enlarged, more-than-human perspective on beauty and value, his work assumes that the other problem of evil cannot be restricted in scope to interhuman affairs. As we saw in "Apology for Bad Dreams," evil's presence and effects extend beyond the interhuman realm to include animals and other more-than-human affairs. This more expansive view of evil takes varied forms in Jeffers's work, and involves consideration of the intentional destruction of the beauties of nature by human beings, the experiencing of suffering by more-than-human beings of various kinds, and the evils that circulate through and among the more-than-human world independent of human presence or genesis. Jeffers speaks to the first sense of evil in the form of the destruction of the natural world in several poems, including such early poems as "The Cycle," which contrasts the "clapping blackness of the wings of pointed cormorants, the great indolent planes / Of autumn pelicans nine or a dozen strung shorelong" with "the hull with standing canvas" that creeps about Point Lobos, and the constant presence of the steamers that "smudge the opal's rim" and the seaplane that "troubles / the sea-wind with its throbbing heart" (CP 1, 14; SP, 22). As these human presences come increasingly to dominate life on earth, Jeffers notes that they will gradually minimize, marginalize, degrade, and eventually extinguish many more-than-human life forms. Observing the ever-further westward march of industry and development during his lifetime, Jeffers poignantly laments the "beautiful places killed like rabbits to make a city [...] my own coast's obscene future" (CP 1, 375; SP, 163). The land surrounding his beloved Tor House—which he describes as being "magnificent unspoiled scenery" upon his arrival in 1914—has by the 1950s been "defaced with a crop of suburban houses" (CP 3, 399; SP, 676).

This unthinking destruction of the beauties and rhythms of the more-than-human world takes on a more intentional, more sinister, and crueler form in many institutionalized human-animal relationships. Echoing the

---

13 Henry David Thoreau, *A Week on the Concord and Merrimack Rivers*, ed. Carl F. Hovde et al. (Princeton, NJ: Princeton University Press, 1980), 77.

rising concern with animal welfare in the radical circles of his own age and anticipating contemporary trends in animal studies, Jeffers is keenly sensitive to animal suffering throughout his *oeuvre* and in his everyday life (it is reported that he refused to hunt or fish). Indeed, in many ways, for Jeffers the existence of widespread animal suffering is one of the chief stumbling blocks standing in the way of a facile affirmation of life, perhaps the prime example of superfluous evil that is difficult to square with the otherwise overwhelming beauty of so much of earthly existence.

All too often, the cause of animal suffering is anthropogenic, such as with the anglers Jeffers describes in his early poem "Salmon Fishing": "pitiful, cruel, primeval" people, who unreflectively draw "landward their live bullion, the bloody mouths / And scales full of the sunset / Twitch on the rocks, no more to wander at will / The wild Pacific pasture nor wanton and spawning / Race up into the fresh water" (CP 1, 6; SP, 22). Human interests are also at the source of the suffering that Jeffers personally witnessed in experiments on laboratory animals, which he recalls in "Memoir":

> […] throat-bandaged dogs cowering in cages, still obsessed with the pitiful
> Love that dogs feel, longing to lick the hand of their devil; and the sick monkeys, dying rats, all sacrificed
> To human inquisitiveness, pedantry, and vanity. (CP 2, 524; SP, 518)

In the lines that follow these, Jeffers goes on to detail watching his friends dehorn cattle and other such cruelties common in human-animal interactions. These mundane forms of violence "make the earth shine like a star with cruelty for light […] this is our world, where only a fool or drunkard makes happy songs" (CP 2, 525; SP, 519).

It would be a mistake, however, to reduce so-called "natural evil" or animal suffering to the evils caused by contemporary human civilization and its institutions. The more-than-human world is filled with its own sources of useless suffering that reside beyond human causes or control. In his narrative work, "Give Your Heart to the Hawks," Jeffers illustrates this point by staging a confrontation between a Bible-thumping father and a son (the protagonist of the drama, Lance Fraser) who has lost his faith. Arguing with his father, Lance uses the example of a deer caught in barbed-wire fencing to decry the pointless cruelties of existence as well as God's failure to intervene to stop them:

> […]The barbs caught him by the loins,
> Across the belly at the spring of the haunches, the top wire.

So there he hangs with his head down, the fore-hooves
Reaching the ground: they dug two trenches in it
Under his suspended nose. That's when he dragged at the barbs
Caught in his belly, his hind legs hacking the air.
No doubt he lived for a week: nothing has touched him: a young
    spike-buck:
A week of torture. What was that for, ah?
D'you think God couldn't see him? The place is very naked and
    open […]
For a loving God, a stinking monument. (CP 2, 351–52; SP, 440–41)

And if we are tempted to find the ultimate cause for the deer's suffering in the erection of fencing by human beings (ultimately making the problem our own), Jeffers would be quick to remind us that suffering and predation are part of the basic fabric of the animal world. In "Steelhead, Wild Pig, the Fungus," for instance, we find a woman, Vina, spearing steelhead in a river, partly for sustenance and partly for entertainment. Hugh Flodden, whose family owns the land through which the river runs, catches Vina in the act of taking fish illegally and makes her pay for the crime by forcing her to have sex with him. Once the sexual act is completed, they spot a group of seagulls nearby fishing in the river and screaming excitedly. Seeing their predatory activities, Vina remarks: "That's a horrible thing[…]. What the birds do. They're worse than I am" (CP 2, 551; SP, 534). Flodden later returns to the river by himself, as if to verify whether Vina's condemnation of the birds holds true, and witnesses a steelhead become trapped and exposed in shallow water, unable to scull back into the deeper currents. Two gulls swoop in and rip the fish's eyes out, leaving it blind and writhing in pain and panic, whereupon a "screaming mob" of seagulls covers the fish and annihilates it. Troubled by the attack, Flodden rides his horse into the birds' midst and scares them off, leaving the fish twitching in agony and struggling for its life. As the birds fly off, their wings cast a fleeting shadow on the suffering below, and Flodden catches sight of "fortune's iniquities." Why should he be "young and happy, mounted on a good horse […] while others have to endure blindness and death / Pain and disease, misery, old age, God knows what worse?" (CP 2, 551; SP, 534).

Reflecting further on the same theme of animal suffering in "Fire on the Hills," Jeffers describes the carnage caused to the resident wildlife by a brush-fire. As the fire races through the mountains, he sees deer bounding ahead of the flames trying to escape death, but recalls that not all animals are as swift. This recognition leads him to consider "the smaller lives that were caught" in the fire, a loss that makes the beauty of the fire as part of a larger ecological whole harder to discern and affirm (as Jeffers notes, "Beauty is not always lovely"). Later, when the fire has passed, Jeffers returns to the burned-out area and catches sight of an eagle who has come a long distance to hunt the few remaining creatures who were able to flee the fire but who will now meet death by other means. Jeffers sees the "sleepily merciless" eagle "perched on the jag of a burnt pine, / Insolent and gorged, cloaked in the folded storms of his shoulders" (CP 2, 173; SP, 394). Despite the manifest beauty and power of natural events, the destruction and suffering they cause can make us question the overall worth of nature and life as a whole.

* * *

I have spent many summer evenings sitting on the beach observing wildlife at Rio del Mar in Aptos, California, just a short distance from where Jeffers lived in Carmel. Looking south from Aptos, one can see the promontory that holds the Point Pinos lighthouse push out into the Pacific Ocean; Jeffers's Tor House is just on the other side of that curve of coastline. On most nights, I see a particular phenomenon that recalls me to his poetry. The event starts an hour or so before sunset. A huge collective of birds—among them pelicans, gulls, murres, and cormorants, numbering in the thousands—gradually starts forming a circular mass that rotates on itself while slowly moving southward. Some birds skim the water, while others land briefly in the middle of the rotating mass. The birds are fishing, collectively and in unison. It is a stunning, undeniably beautiful display, with birds so numerous they darken the sky above you if you are anywhere near them in the water during the event. The whole thing appears to be carefully choreographed, with the birds skillfully avoiding striking one another, and their collective feeding carried out with the utmost precision and efficiency. Yet, one cannot help reflect on the panic and terror of the fish below the water that remain hidden from human view. The suffering and death that occur in the ocean on those evenings are unthinkable in scope, with mackerel, anchovies, smelt, and perch suffering and dying by the hundreds of thousands. And this play of life and death that forms the ocean's trophic chains has recurred for eons before we arrived and will continue until the oceans are someday exhausted and can no longer sustain the birds above or the fish and other forms of life below.

It would, perhaps, be consolatory to believe that only human beings produce terrible suffering and that we are a temporary anomaly in the earth's history, a late-arriving and soon-to-be extinct species of animal that represents an aberration in an otherwise beautiful and majestic story of cosmic unfolding and planetary evolution. To be sure, Jeffers is himself tempted to console himself and his readers in this way (a theme I will take up at more length in subsequent chapters). But his best poems resist this temptation, and they consistently acknowledge that the other problem of evil is not simply an interhuman problem but inheres in the very fabric of life. In "Birds and Fishes," for example, Jeffers paints a scene of destruction and killing that is much like the one I have just described. He refers to the millions of fish that swim past his edge of the coastline and how they attract the mass of birds at feeding time. He characterizes the birds' feeding as a "festival," motivated by "envy and malice" and "hysterical greed." The mob-hysteria of the birds, he notes, is "nearly human—these decent birds!—as if they were finding / Gold in the street." The frenzy of feeding activity leads Jeffers to ponder: "Which one in all this fury of wildfowl pities the fish? / No one certainly. Justice and mercy / Are human dreams, they do not concern the birds nor the fish nor eternal God" (CP 3, 426; SP, 687).

* * *

I have cataloged this litany of human and more-than-human evils in Jeffers's poetry not to paint an overly pessimistic portrait either of his work or of the nature of existence as such. Rather, the point here is to underscore the importance of the task of coming to grips with the difficulties and dark sides of existence in the context of a life lived entirely within an immanent frame. As I try to demonstrate in the following chapters, Jeffers's poetry suggests that one of the chief tasks of the poet today is to offer reasons to believe in this world (to borrow a notion from Gilles Deleuze) in the face of painful realities that can all-too-easily lead us to turn away from it in disgust and despair. As Jeffers notes in commenting on "Apology for Bad Dreams," although "cruelty is a part of nature [...] it is the one thing that seems unnatural to us" (CP 4, 394; SP, 717). As we have seen in this chapter, though, for Jeffers cruelty and evil are *entirely* natural. Thus, if we accept and "recognize cruelty and evil as part of the sum of things" (CP 4, 394; SP, 717), as Jeffers suggests we must, we are faced with the challenge of articulating how and whether life can be lived and affirmed in the face of such recognition.

Chapter 2

SAVIORS

In the opening pages of *Civilization and Its Discontents* (1930), Sigmund Freud offers what has become one of the most influential accounts of the origins of religion and religious-based civilizations.[1] Pushing back against his friend and interlocutor Romain Rolland, who argues that religion arises in response to an "oceanic" feeling latent in all human beings,[2] Freud insists that the phenomenon of religious belief (at least for the common person) is grounded in the much more basic fact of human vulnerability. "Life, as we find it," Freud suggests, "is too hard for us; it brings us too many pains, disappointments, and impossible tasks."[3] In response to the difficulties of existence, Freud believes we turn to religion (and here Freud has in mind primarily popular forms of the Christian religion) for salvation and consolation. Religion, he tells us, promises a comprehensive explanation of our condition and assures us that a providential father figure is watching over our lives and will ensure a good end for us. On Freud's analysis, religion thus serves as one of a host of "palliative measures"[4] we use to deal with the hardships of daily life. Further, he believes that civilization itself emerges as one of the chief means whereby we seek to alleviate and prevent suffering. By living and working together in larger groups, conforming to social norms, and submitting to rulers, governments, police, and other state apparatuses, we seek to adjust our relations with nature and our fellow human beings such that our pain is minimized and daily existence is rendered as comfortable and pleasurable as possible.

That the establishment of civilization as a solution to the problem of existence creates a whole host of unintended discontents of its own is, of course,

---

1 Sigmund Freud, *Civilization and Its Discontents*, trans. James Strachey (New York: W. W. Norton, 1961).
2 Rolland is commenting on Freud's theses on religion as presented in a small book Freud published in 1927 (just prior to the publication of *Civilization and Its Discontents*) entitled *The Future of an Illusion*, trans. James Strachey (New York: W. W. Norton, 1961).
3 Freud, *Civilization and Its Discontents*, 22.
4 Freud, *Civilization and Its Discontents*, 22.

Freud's central cultural-psychoanalytic insight. Modern civilizations, especially the highly religious kind that dominate in Western culture, place excessive normative demands on individuals in regard to their sexual and social lives; the struggle to meet such demands, Freud argues, splinters the psyche and gives rise to the formation of a super-ego and to the persistent discontent of living under the surveillance of an internal watchman.[5] These unanticipated and unintended consequences of the development of our religious civilization pose what Freud believes is the key question that faces human beings in the coming generations: namely, how to bring the demands of civilization more into line with the psychic health and happiness of the individuals who constitute it.

Jeffers's reflections on the "evils" and hardships of daily existence that we examined in Chapter 1 are, as should be evident, quite similar to those that form the focus of Freud's analysis. Both Jeffers and Freud view human beings as vulnerable creatures who often experience a preponderance of suffering throughout their lives. They also share the notion that this condition must be addressed if human beings are to achieve any kind of life worth living. Where Jeffers and Freud depart from each other is at the level of prognosis. How, precisely, should human beings work with and through their earthly condition in order to flourish and achieve some kind of psychic and social integrity? While, as we have just noted, Freud believes that the turn toward civilization as a means of dealing with the challenges of life is an imperfect solution, he ultimately believes that the most effective way of dealing with our individual and collective discontent lies further down the path of civilizational development and reform. As we will see Jeffers has, by contrast, a far more pessimistic and critical account of civilization, which leads him to suggest that any genuine solution to the problems of the human condition requires an extra- or post-civilizational orientation that moves us not simply in the direction of the individual or toward anarchism but rather beyond an exclusive focus on interhuman affairs.

Beyond Civilization, Beyond Saviors

To understand how Jeffers arrives at this conclusion, let's first examine more carefully his own reflections on the human tendency to turn toward religious and political saviors for consolation. In one of his earliest poems on the topic, "Point Pinos and Point Lobos," we find Jeffers initially commending Jesus for his attempts to help human beings ameliorate the challenging aspects of their condition; he likewise refuses to mock the religious impulse of believers

---

5 Freud, *Civilization and Its Discontents*, 71.

and their desire for salvation, suggesting that in some ways he is among them. Jeffers does, however, ultimately reject Christianity and other religions of pity (Buddhism is his primary example in this poem)—not because they attempt to help human beings with their struggles, but because he believes they effectively turn us away from this world and from the basic structures and cycles that make up reality.

The fundamental structure of reality is characterized here by Jeffers using the classical image of the *rota Fortunae*, or "Wheel of Fortune," made famous in Western literature by Boethius's *The Consolation of Philosophy*. In that text, the figure of Lady Philosophy consoles the imprisoned Boethius by encouraging him to turn his gaze away from the vicissitudes of Fortune and toward the deeper, more stable, and more rational order established by Providence.[6] Jeffers suggests that the world religions would have us do much the same thing as Lady Philosophy: disavow and avert our gaze from the fundamental structures and cycles of this world and redirect our attention to another world that lies beyond that of finite, mortal experience.

But no such escape is possible on Jeffers's account; all things and individuals—including Jesus and Buddha themselves—are strapped to the Wheel of Fortune and will share the same fate. Referring perhaps to his reading of Nietzsche's *Thus Spoke Zarathustra* when he was a young man,[7] Jeffers recalls that someone

> Whispered into my ear when I was very young, some serpent whispered
> That what has gone returns; what has been, is; what will be, was; the future
> Is a farther past; our times he said fractions of arcs of the great circle;
> And the wheel turns, nothing shall stop it nor destroy it, we are bound on the wheel,
> We and the stars and seas, the mountains and the Buddha. (CP 1, 96–97)

---

6 Lady Philosophy reminds Boethius that "Fortune, of course, is a monster, and she toys with those for whom she intends catastrophe, showing her friendly face and lifting them up before dashing them down when they are least prepared for it […] . To the cries and complaints of men she pays no mind whatever." By contrast, God is "goodness itself […] and he orders all things for the good, inasmuch as he orders all things and he is good" (Boethius, *The Consolation of Philosophy*, trans. David R. Slavitt [Cambridge, MA: Harvard University Press, 2008], 27, 30, 100).

7 See CL 1, 768. Jeffers openly acknowledges the influence of Nietzsche on his poetry (CL 3, 596) but denies that his work is simply derived from Nietzsche's ideas (CL 1, 690). This passage also echoes Ecclesiastes 3:15, which Jeffers would have also read when he was "very young."

This fundamentally "pagan" view of the world as a series of recurring cycles—which Jeffers borrows in part from Nietzsche as well as from ancient Hellenistic sources and contemporary philosophical and scientific accounts of nature—is in many ways a challenging and austere one, and it offers no guarantee that things are ordered in a way that will prove beneficial to human beings. On this view of the world, there is no definite point in time in which creation takes place, no eschaton, no redemption, and no Sovereign to guarantee that the cosmos will unfold according to an inner *logos*. But Jeffers's poetic project is committed to the notion that those who can fully behold and affirm the more austere, cyclical vision of reality can eventually achieve happiness and will in fact desire to "praise it to the people" (CP 1, 98).

One of the primary obstacles lying in the way of beholding and affirming this vision of reality is that it demands a radical decentering of human beings and a downgrading of the high value that traditional religions tend to grant to human existence. On this point, too, Freud and Jeffers are aligned. Freud generally believes that religion, by elevating the importance of human beings in the planetary and cosmic scheme of things, functions as a sop to human narcissism.[8] The Judeo-Christian tradition in particular, Freud argues, grants human beings a central place in the larger planetary and cosmic orders and endeavors to reassure us that our conscious subjectivity and individual agency render us unique and significant. The "severe blows" delivered to this version of human narcissism by the scientific advances of Copernicus and a long line of previous astronomers (who undercut our sense of cosmic centrality and importance), Charles Darwin (who shatters our sense of biological uniqueness), and Freud himself (who, along with philosophers like Arthur Schopenhauer, demonstrate that "*the ego is not master in its own house*") should eventually, Freud suggests, serve to usher in a more modest and honest picture of the human condition.[9] As we have noted, Freud is not naïve about the swiftness with which such changes might occur or the general unwillingness of human beings to face their condition (the latter, in fact, is the chief "difficulty" that lies in the "path" of psychoanalysis); but any successful negotiation of that condition requires, he believes, a forthright assessment of its fundamental nature.

Jeffers shares this critical approach to human narcissism and maintains that we have been taught by religious and political saviors to guard

---

8 Sigmund Freud, "A Difficulty in the Path of Psycho-analysis," in *The Standard Edition of the Complete Psychological Works of Sigmund Freud*, ed. James Strachey, vol. 17 (London: Hogarth, 1955), 137–44.
9 Freud, "A Difficulty in the Path of Psycho-analysis," 139–43.

ourselves from the brute facts of the human condition. Part of the task of genuine poetry, Jeffers believes, is to be forthright about our condition and not to falsely elevate or flatter ourselves (as he believes many previous poets have done).[10] To this end, he notes in "Quia Absurdum" (CP 3, 213; SP, 591) that we have been encouraged to look away from "the terrible empty light of space, the bottomless / Pool of the stars"; further, we have learned to disavow the "inherent nastiness of man and woman" and adopt an overly optimistic portrait of human nature. For Jeffers, whether we choose the "Christian sheep-cote / Or the Communist rat fight," our "faith" will encourage us to cover our heads "from the man-devouring stars."

If we were, by contrast, to risk exposing ourselves to these uncomfortable truths, we might, Jeffers believes, learn something important not just about the human condition but about how to live well *within* that condition. That said, Jeffers is not altogether unsympathetic to the general inclination people have to turn away from hard truths. His approach to confronting life's challenges is not that of a paternalistic Stoic who grabs us by the scruff of the neck and demands that we look at reality without buffers or mediation. He acknowledges that it is hard to stand on one's own in the midst of life's difficulties; and he openly confesses to his own temptations to flee authentic living and follow others, both in his poetic work and in his life direction more generally. For it is in truth far easier, and frankly far more reasonable, to fall back on leaders, tradition, and heritage in determining how to live than it is to strike out on one's own or enter into a collective experiment in living differently.

For those of us who have been raised in a culture that prioritizes the values of spontaneity and novelty, it might be tempting to mock such conservative attitudes toward tradition and leaders. To do so, though, would be to misunderstand the gravity of finding oneself in a situation where tradition and leaders have gone missing. Like Jeffers, we live in an age where social institutions have been largely eviscerated, including at the micro-level of the family, the meso-level of neighborhoods and communities, and at the macro-level of larger state, national, and international relations. To celebrate facilely such breakdown as an opportunity for creating society entirely anew is to confuse

---

10 Jeffers traces this decision not to tell lies in his poetry back to Nietzsche, citing Nietzsche's remark from Part II of *Thus Spoke Zarathustra*: "The poets lie too much" (see CP 4, 391). Nietzsche is himself echoing a host of previous philosophers who raise the same issue, including Plutarch (*De audiendis poetis*, 16a ff.) and Aristotle, who notes in his *Metaphysics* that "bards tell many a lie" (983a). The question of the honesty of poets is also at issue in Plato's consideration of the "ancient quarrel" between philosophy and poetry that I discuss in the Introduction.

the importance of adopting an experimental attitude toward life with the necessary and minimal conditions under which such experimentation can be fruitfully carried out (a point that the experimental philosopher par excellence, Michel de Montaigne, underscores). Indeed, finding ourselves in circumstances where the reconstitution of individual and social existence must occur whole cloth and from the ground up can be an overwhelming burden, and it is certainly nothing to be naively invoked or celebrated.

Yet, on Jeffers's analysis, such a situation is (for better or for worse) where we have found ourselves. In terms of the prospects of leaders or the heritage of Western civilization providing us with the tools to address the problems we face, Jeffers believes our prospects are dim. We have inherited a culture that is deeply unsustainable and clearly in decline, and the dominant models of religion and leadership that are on offer within it are simply not up to the task of extricating us from the existential difficulties in which we find ourselves. Jeffers's task as a poet and a thinker is to help us appreciate this conundrum, to seek a way out of the dead-end at which Western culture has arrived, and to strive to live well and live through this limit by charting another path.

Jeffers's reasons for believing that our leaders and traditions can no longer provide us with answers to the basic existential questions of life are several. First of all, he suggests that our leaders have repeatedly proven they lack the fortitude to be genuine leaders. In "Intellectuals" (CP 2, 283), Jeffers reiterates the difficulty of the average person living without guidance, querying rhetorically whether it is really "so hard for men to stand by themselves, / They must hang on Marx or Christ, or mere Progress? / Clearly it is hard." But he goes on to emphasize that the same difficulty plagues the leaders themselves. They "ought to be leaders," he states, but when "Night comes, and the wolves of doubt" arrive, they lose their nerve and return to the fold. Leaders should, ideally, be advance scouts for the people and travel alone "through long thoughts to redeeming despair" in order to determine the direction to be taken and the values to be upheld. But when the time comes for these decisions to be made, and assurances and signposts are lacking, the leaders become "tired and cover their eyes; they flock into the fold."

One should be reminded here of the social and political events through which Jeffers himself lived, when the leaders of his own country advocated for the easy, familiar path of undertaking wars of choice and stoking nationalist prejudices instead of learning to live within their means and addressing their unjust relations with the land and with its exploited people. That our contemporary leaders have continued down this same path goes, perhaps, without saying, but we should nevertheless note that Jeffers's remarks about the lack of fortitude among leaders are by no means outmoded in our own time. In the face of unprecedented challenges arising across multiple registers—from economic to political to ecological—our leaders still default to platitudes about national greatness, democracy, and market-based solutions, a gesture that allows leaders themselves and their constituents to continue to live their status quo lives and to ignore the pressing need for fundamental change at all levels of individual and collective existence.

Jeffers's point here, though, is not simply to chastise or shame leaders in the hope that they will do their jobs more conscientiously. Rather, his point is that leaders in general are not the visionaries we believe them to be but are primarily intent upon securing and maintaining their own power. In a blistering critique of communist political leadership entitled "Blind Horses" (CP 2, 519),[11] Jeffers suggests that even when the masses try to cast off leaders ("The proletariat for your Messiah, the poor and many are to seize power and make the world new"), rulers make their return under the purported need to help organize resistance and sustain the momentum of the revolution. And once they are again in power, their "first duty" is "to defend their power;" and what leaders "defend / To-day they will love to-morrow; it becomes theirs, their property." Jeffers goes on to remark that just as Lenin served the revolution, Stalin is betraying it: "For the sake of power, the Party's power, the state's / Power, armed power, Stalin's power." Here Jeffers links Stalin's politics with what he calls "Caesarean power."

The link between Stalin and Caesar is meant to recall the reader, of course, to the fact that the social formation being ushered in by the communist revolution at that time is, despite appearances, "not quite a new world." Demagogues who claim to represent the poor and disenfranchised have long "massed and moulded" these groups to their own ends. Jeffers knew his classical history well. He had read and reread the ancient historians on the political machinations of the Roman rulers Sulla,[12] Pompey, and Caesar, how the noble political ideals of the Republic were betrayed by leaders who often initially had strong support from their own people, and how they gained that support by apportioning "food and labor and amusement," or in Juvenal's apt phrase, "bread and circuses" for the people.[13] Whether this pattern of betrayal and power grabs by leaders is inevitable is beyond Jeffers's purview of course, but he insists rightly that it is all too common. In a line added at the last minute to the page proofs of "Blind Horses" (a line that also gave Jeffers

---

11 Tim Hunt notes that earlier drafts of the poem were titled "Marxian Parenthesis" and "Karl Marx and his World" (CP 5, 580).
12 See, for example, "The Broken Balance" (CP 1, 372–76; SP, 160–64).
13 Juvenal, *Satires*, 10.80.

the final title for the poem), he queries: "The ages like blind horses turning a mill tread their own hoof marks. / Whose corn's ground in that mill?"

Beyond the Individual

If Jeffers is read in a cursory fashion, his criticisms of religious saviors and political leaders might seem to point toward a kind of individualist anarchism as the solution to the problems of life within civilization. After all, if religious and political leaders divert us from the truth of the human condition; if they recurrently end up parroting the decadent tendencies of the masses; and if they inevitably become the worst sorts of demagogues, it is reasonable to conclude that the solution to our problems is to turn our backs on leaders of all sorts and rely on ourselves as individuals. We might even conclude that civilization itself, with its outmoded norms and commitment to Statecraft, is the problem. Freud's analysis, as we have seen, highlights this tension between individual autonomy and the opposing demands of civilized living; and he anticipates the conclusion that some readers will draw that the way out of the horns of this dilemma is to take the side of individual autonomy and happiness over and against that of the welfare of the collective. While sympathetic to this sort of individualism, Freud ultimately rejects it as a viable solution to the human condition. We have formed large-scale civilizations, he argues, precisely because this sort of individualist approach to life outside the state proves too hard for most human animals. The benefits that large-scale civilization and governments bring to individuals, from this evolutionary-historical perspective, outweigh its drawbacks. For Freud, then, the only rational way forward is to acknowledge the benefits and superiority of civilization over individualism and then work to reform and ameliorate civilization's irrational and unhealthy tendencies (many of which, Freud believes, stem from its religious roots).

Jeffers appears to adopt the opposite tack by experimenting with individualist solutions to the problems of civilization and its saviors in many of his early narrative poems, most notably "The Women at Point Sur" (CP 1, 240–367). Here, Rev. Dr. Barclay (whom we saw in the last chapter announce the death of God to his parishioners), when freed from the illusions of religion and from having Christ as his exemplar, decides to found his own religion. The central premise of Barclay's religion is that the traditional Judeo-Christian commandments no longer hold and that we are entirely free to experiment with our own norms and ways of life. Barclay takes such post-religious freedom to its limit, paying women for sex and eventually even raping his own daughter. Although Jeffers places many of his own ideas in Barclay's mouth and uses this character to expose the limits of the religious faith in which he was reared, at the same time he clearly aims to show the dead-end of Barclay's penchant for transgression for transgression's sake. In general, the fundamental problem of modern life for Jeffers does not seem to be simply that of the individual versus the collective; nor are genuine meaning and freedom to be found simply in pursuing individual license. Instead, what Jeffers seems most interested in exploring in "The Women at Point Sur" and other early narratives of similar sorts (such as "Tamar" and "Roan Stallion") are the various routes that his main characters chart in "breaking out of humanity" (CL 1, 689). It is in these narratives and in the imaginative poetic experiments with post-human living that Jeffers finds the requisite space for thinking about what it means to be human after the death of the Judeo-Christian God and in view of the failure of human saviors more generally to provide genuine consolation and a meaningful life.

Jeffers maintains that, on the other side of the human and beyond the scope of both individual concern and interhuman affairs, there is an inhuman world—one that he will sometimes risk calling "God"—that is very much worth reverencing. The narrator of "Intellectuals" reminds himself that "if you had not encountered and loved / Our unkindly all but inhuman God [...] You too might have been looking about for a church" (CP 2, 283). Even though this poem is crafted in such a way as to encourage the reader to assume that moving beyond reliance on "Marx or Christ, or mere Progress" is the beginning of a turn toward individual freedom, the narrator ultimately rejects self-reliance (in the colloquial if not Emersonian sense) and ends up turning instead to God for salvation. To be sure, this is not the God of the mainstream Judeo-Christian tradition, in whom belief is no longer possible for either Nietzsche or Jeffers.[14] Nor is this the God of any of the major world religions. If Jeffers's inhuman God has any proximate correlate, it can perhaps be found in Spinoza's *Deus sive Natura* (God, or Nature), where the two words (God and Nature) are simply different names for the same subject.[15]

---

14 "The greatest recent event—that 'God is dead,' that the belief in the Christian god has become unbelievable—is already beginning to cast its first shadows over Europe" (Friedrich Nietzsche, *The Gay Science: With a Prelude in Rhymes and an Appendix of Songs*, trans. Walter Kaufmann [New York: Vintage Books, 1974], 279). I should underscore that I have here written "mainstream" Judeo-Christian tradition. In the conclusion, I will suggest that Jeffers's God is in fact very much like the inhuman God of the biblical book of Job—a God who can be rightly said to "belong" to the Judeo-Christian tradition but who, despite his canonical status, remains very much in the margins of that tradition.

15 See CL 2, 34 for Jeffers's invocation of Spinoza's notion of God. Arthur B. Coffin explores the Jeffers-Spinoza connection at more length in *Robinson Jeffers: Poet of Inhumanism* (Madison, WI: University of Wisconsin Press, 1977) 253–57. See also the

God, in Jeffers's poetry, is but one name among others for the sum total of relatively permanent and permanently recurring forces, energies, and relations that constitute the planet and the cosmos, somewhat akin to Spinoza's *Natura naturans*. This God, this Nature is "all but inhuman" and essentially impersonal.

Yet, for the narrator of "Intellectuals," this God (or Nature) is also "very beautiful" and worthy of our deepest admiration and loyalty. And here is where we gain a glimpse of the larger stakes of Jeffers's approach. To underscore a point mentioned at the beginning of this chapter, Jeffers is not at all denigrating the philosophico-religious *impulse*. The desire to find meaning in life and ways of living in a worthwhile manner are, for Jeffers, fundamental to the human condition and essential for overcoming pessimism. The difference between Jeffers's approach and that of the more common kind of post-religious and secular approach we have been examining in Freud is that Jeffers believes this desire can only be fulfilled in a lasting way by turning our love outward, beyond the confines of human civilization to the inhuman, more-than-human world.[16] It is our human narcissism and anthropocentrism, in other words, that are blocking access to the path to salvation and consolation. These latter ends can only be accomplished, Jeffers insists, in and through the inhuman cosmos itself and in our establishing a different disposition toward that cosmos and our place in it.

Jeffers develops this inhumanist reorientation at more length in his "Meditation on Saviors," a poem that contains *in nuce* his critical analysis of saviorism as well as his alternative vision for salvation. Salvation, Jeffers suggests here, ultimately comes by force to all of us through death, an event in which individual consciousness is extinguished and the body is gradually reintegrated into the elements.[17] Through death, we become one (once again) with the inhuman world. But becoming-inhuman can also be achieved while we are alive if we learn to "make health" in our minds and practice love of "the coast opposite humanity" (CP 1, 401; SP, 77). Through the practice of

---

deep ecologist George Sessions's influential article on this topic, "Spinoza and Jeffers on Man in Nature," *Inquiry* 20 (1977): 481–528.

16 Freud offers an essentially pragmatic and utilitarian account of how human beings find meaning in life and ways to endure suffering, arguing that given the variation in psychological constitution among individuals, we need a variety of ways to deal with life's challenges. His fundamental objection to religion along these lines is that it restricts this varied "play of choice and adaptation" (Freud, *Civilization and Its Discontents*, 31).

17 I take up the issue of Jeffers's approach to death and dying at more length in Chapter 5.

learning to love beyond ourselves and beyond the narrow confines of interhuman relations, we are freed of the anxious and unhealthy love that renders life "less lovely [...] a little troublesome, a little terrible" (CP 1, 396; SP, 172). In this way, we take the narrow form of love that typically orients our lives and lay it out

> like bread on the waters; [love] is worst turned inward, it is best shot farthest.
> Love, the mad wine of good and evil, the saint's and murderer's, the mote in the eye that makes its object
> Shine the sun black; the trap in which it is better to catch the inhuman God than the hunter's own image. (CP 1, 401; SP, 77)

***

My aim in the following chapters is to examine this vision of inhumanism at more length and to consider the various components comprised under this notion. But before taking up this task, and as a means of concluding the present chapter, it would behoove us briefly to consider the political implications of Jeffers's rejection of saviors and his predilection for more-than-human existence. Jeffers's sharp denunciation of traditional religion and established political programs has made it difficult for critics to position him in terms of his broader ideological commitments. The tendency among critics has been to assume that if Jeffers rejects a given position, he must be committed to its opposite (e.g., if Marxism is criticized, this implies an endorsement of capitalism; if Christianity is rejected, this implies a commitment to atheism).[18] In this vein, as Alex Vardamis notes, Jeffers has been accused by critics of "fascism, communism, anarchism, pacifism, isolationism, sadism, misanthropy, and atheism"—and that's just the short list.[19]

Now, clearly, one cannot be committed to all of these positions at once; so rather than trying to refute each accusation and attribution in turn, it might

---

18 Jeffers comments on this (il)logic in a letter to Leo Wolfson (CL 3, 431).
19 See Alex A. Vardamis, "Robinson Jeffers: Poet of Controversy," in *Centennial Essays for Robinson Jeffers*, ed. Robert Zaller (Newark, NJ: University of Delaware Press, 1999), 44–67, citation at 44. For another list of accusations and an alternative way of assessing Jeffers's political orientation, see Edward A. Nickerson, "The Politics of Robinson Jeffers," in *Centennial Essays for Robinson Jeffers*, ed. Robert Zaller (Newark, NJ: University of Delaware Press, 1999), 254–67. I return to the issue of Jeffers's politics in Chapter 5.

be more helpful to consider the question of Jeffers's politics from a different angle, one that does not seek to place him on this sort of grid of familiar political coordinates. And if, in fact, the reading of Jeffers we are pursuing here (one that stresses the displacement of anthropocentrism as one of his overarching concerns) hits the mark, it should be evident why standard ideological coordinates do little to illuminate the sorts of political stands he might take or the particular values he seems to espouse: namely, nearly all of the dominant spiritual and political ideologies (especially in the Western tradition) are strongly centered on interhuman affairs. As a consequence, any perspective or set of practices and values that decenters human beings and interhuman affairs is bound to make for an ill fit with those ideologies. This is certainly the case with Jeffers's project. In rejecting the absolute primacy and importance of interhuman affairs, he has effectively exited the political and spiritual conversation as it is carried out by the established order. Of course, this does not mean that there are no values or politics that might correspond to inhumanism; there most certainly are, and I will have much more to say about the normative dimensions of inhumanism in subsequent chapters. But in order to appreciate this alternative vision, it is necessary to suspend temporarily our typical ways of thinking about normative matters and to be willing to rethink in a fundamental way the sources and scope of norms as well as what form a worthwhile way of life might take once we adopt an inhumanist perspective.

Chapter 3

COSMOS

> Protagoras was really and truly having us on when he made 'Man the measure of all things'—Man, who has never really known his own measurements.
>
> —*Michel de Montaigne*[1]

The Nature of Things

"The poets lie too much"—except, perhaps, the ancient Roman poet Titus Lucretius Carus. Although he admits to rimming the cup of his lessons with honey to take some of the edge off his austere message, Lucretius sees it as his task in his six-book poem, *De rerum natura*, to provide readers with a forthright and truthful account of the cosmos and the place of human beings within it. As a disciple of the early Greek philosopher Epicurus, Lucretius maintains that our anxieties about life and fears surrounding death are due to patently false superstitions about vengeful gods intent on causing trouble for us in this life and in the afterlife. The aim of philosophy as Lucretius sees it is to dispel "our terrors and our darknesses of mind" by giving us "insight into nature" and a schema of "systematic contemplation" that can help us understand who we really are and how the world truly works.[2]

On Lucretius's account, the universe is constituted only by material particles and the void of empty space. The individual things we see around us are comprised of such particles of varied sizes and sorts and are brought together by chance to form relatively stable (but not invariant) patterns of existence and relation. While the individuals, groups, and patterns that form in nature and the cosmos are subject to change and destruction, the particles

---

[1] Michel de Montaigne, *An Apology for Raymond Sebond*, trans. and ed. M. A. Screech (New York: Penguin 1987), 136.
[2] Lucretius, *The Way Things Are*, trans. Rolfe Humphries (Bloomington, IN: Indiana University Press, 1968), 24 (I.146–49).

themselves are indestructible. Human souls are also, according to Lucretius, built from these same particles and, hence, are subject to the same processes of constitution and destruction. Our souls do not survive us after death and thus cannot be subject to punishment by the gods for anything we do in this life. Furthermore, if there are any gods, they would, Lucretius believes, be utterly uninterested in human affairs. The gods control neither the constitution and destruction of assembled particles nor the vicissitudes of human affairs; both realms unfold according to largely deterministic forces as well as random swerves from that predictable order. Thus, there is no Providence to ensure that any given pattern of existence or kind of being will persist or fare well, least of all human civilization or individual human beings. As Lucretius maintains: "to think that gods / Have organized all things for the sake of men / Is nothing but a lot of foolishness."[3] Human beings can achieve some measure of happiness and tranquility in life, however, if we understand these matters clearly and observe some basic practices that help us to affirm and align our daily lives with the basic nature of things.

Jeffers is, in many ways, "our" Lucretius—not in the sense of offering us an updated form of Lucretian Epicureanism but rather in taking up the perennial philosophical and spiritual tasks that motivated Lucretius's poetry: to dispel our anxieties and fears about death, to offer us consolation in the face of the difficulties of existence, and to do so not through flattery or foolish notions about our importance in the bigger scheme of things but through an honest picture of the nature of things and our place in and among them. And just as Lucretius sought to base his philosophy on a resolutely materialistic and scientific view of the nature of things, so too does Jeffers insist on thinking and writing poetry in view of the modern scientific and cosmological revolutions that have radically altered our understanding of the nature of things.[4]

Indeed, the very first poem Jeffers published as a 16-year old, "The Measure" (CP 4, 1), already indicates his desire to place his thinking within a modern cosmological perspective and to have that perspective reframe human life and its significance. In this early lyric, the young Jeffers takes

---

3 Lucretius, *The Way Things Are*, 56–57 (II.174–76).
4 Referring to "the importance of science for the artist and for the thinker," Jeffers writes in a 1937 letter to Hyatt Howe Waggoner: "It seems to me that for the thinker (in the wider sense of the word) a scientific basis is an essential condition. We cannot take any philosophy seriously if it ignores or garbles the knowledge and view-points that determine the intellectual life of our time." As for the artist, Jeffers notes that "science is important but not all essential. He might have no more modern science than Catallus yet be as great an artist. But his range and significance would be limited accordingly" (CL 1, 769–770). In a similar vein, Jeffers describes himself in response to a questionnaire as bearing a "mechanistic anti-spiritual point of view from medical school, running in harness with a mysticism that seems almost instinctive" (CP 4, 553).

issue with Protagoras's dictum that "Man is the measure of all things: of the things which are, that they are, and of the things which are not, that they are not."[5] For Jeffers, the notions that human beings might be the measure of things, and that the earth on which we live is the world or "cosmos" as a whole (or is at least at the center of it), belong to an irretrievably ancient and outmoded perspective. Modern astronomy has shown us "the depths of space," a perspective which decenters earth and makes its importance and greatness abate. Likewise, the enlarged cosmos in which we find ourselves decenters human beings, making us look like "worms upon a little clod" when placed against the backdrop of the "greater measure" of deep space.

As we will see in the present chapter, such references to cosmic space, deep time, and related phenomena only intensify in Jeffers's mature poetry; and the use of astronomical and cosmological themes in his work mark more than just a passing personal interest in astronomical matters. As part of his daily routine at Tor House, just before retiring to bed, Jeffers would walk outside to gaze into the night sky and study the stars. This ritual practice gave him intimate knowledge of the constellations and created in his patterns of thinking and living a habitual sense of astronomical perspective and cosmic time. Yet Jeffers's understanding of astronomy and cosmology went well beyond that of an amateur enthusiast, due in part to his familiarity with the work of his younger brother, Hamilton Moore Jeffers. Hamilton, who was six years Robinson's junior, was a professional astrometrist with a PhD in astronomy from UC Berkeley. Hamilton spent the bulk of his career at Lick Observatory (located at Mt. Hamilton, California, less than one hundred miles away from Tor House in Carmel) measuring the positions of comets, asteroids, and other astronomical phenomena. We are not entirely sure how much Jeffers knew of his brother's work, but cosmological and astronomical themes discussed throughout his mature poetry make it clear that he was paying careful attention to the latest scientific developments related to Hamilton's research and doing so with considerable sophistication and understanding.

Jeffers also happened to live during an era in which a series of major advances in cosmology took place, and he had his own front-row seat to many of them through his personal relationship with another astronomer, Edwin Hubble.[6] Hubble's transformational discoveries about the size of the universe and the motion of nebulae during the early twentieth century had a profound effect on Jeffers's work; and this influence is on clear display in several of the

---

5 Plato attributes this statement to Protagoras in *Theaetetus*, 152a.
6 To my knowledge, no one has written about the nature or extent of this relationship, but letters record that the families socialized together on occasion, that Edwin Hubble and Hamilton were friends, and that Jeffers kept up with Hubble's research.

poems that were written around the time of these discoveries. In one such work, "Margrave" (originally published in 1931), Jeffers seeks to bring the intellectual shifts in cosmic perspective provided by cosmology to bear on the practical affairs of mundane human actions. By bringing such "far separated things into affinity" (CL 2, 84)—in the instance of "Margrave," it is a matter of bringing together the astronomical discovery of the "flight of the nebulae" and the kinds of sordid crimes reported regularly in the news[7]—Jeffers sought to recast the significance of human existence and human consciousness by placing them in an ever-widening cosmic context. Echoing themes in his early poem "The Measure," Jeffers remarks in the opening stanzas of "Margrave" that "The earth was the world and man was its measure, but our minds have looked / Through the little mock-dome of heaven the telescope-slotted observatory eye-ball, there space and multitude came in / And the earth is a particle of dust by a sand-grain sun, lost in a nameless cove of the shores of a continent" (CP 2, 160; SP, 382).

Jeffers goes on to note in "Margrave" that the "learned astronomer / Analyzing the light of most remote star-swirls / Has found them—or a trick of distance deludes his prism—/ All at incredible speed fleeing outward from ours" (CP 2, 161; SP, 383). The "ours" from which the nebulae are fleeing are, of course, the stars of our galaxy—and even closer to home, the human consciousnesses that populate earth. From the cosmic perspective that Jeffers often adopted, consciousness appears to be an anomaly and sort of curse, something from which the stars are metaphorically fleeing out of fear of contagion. Consciousness is our "distinction perhaps," Jeffers writes, but "hardly an advantage." It makes us "slaver for contemptible pleasures / And scream with pain" (CP 2, 160; SP, 382). In "Margarve," the status and place of human beings in the expanded cosmic scheme of things remains obscure. Our newfound awareness of the vastness and inhumanness of the cosmos seems to resist our efforts to reposition ourselves within it and to render *us* alien (rather than the other way around). To a certain extent, we seem to be beings set apart, beings who bring the "world to focus" in our awakened consciousness and thereby interrupt the "sonambulism of nature" (CP 2, 160; SP, 382), but we do so only to our distinct disadvantage and largely in the service of trivial pleasures.

The way through and beyond this ambiguity concerning the human condition, for Jeffers, lies in recognizing that consciousness is neither a genuine human distinctive (he suggests in several places that it is present in degrees

---

7 Jeffers is here referring to the case of William Edward Hickman, who kidnapped and murdered a 12-year-old girl at the time. For fuller details, see CL 2, 84, n. 2.

throughout the more-than-human world[8]) nor is it limited to serving our merely utilitarian interests. This "net of nerves" we happen to have also, on occasion, "catches the splendor of things" (CP 2, 160; SP, 382) and thereby allows us to open onto and become something more than just human, something beyond the distinctives on which we often (misguidedly) pride ourselves. It would not be an overstatement to say that Jeffers's poetry is ultimately dedicated to this task of catching sight of and remaining with the splendor of things (to whatever degree possible). But—and here is the rub—persisting with the "splendor" and "unbridled beauty" of things is not something easily accomplished. It requires a protracted *askēsis*, or discipline, a sustained and habitual effort to become something other than who we are. Through sustained practice of this sort, we learn to see consistently from a more cosmic, more inhuman perspective and thereby become more inhuman ourselves.

As If for the First Time

The basic coordinates of this transformative path are sketched out in Jeffers's 1923 lyric "Continent's End," a piece that was in large part responsible for his initially gaining the attention of critics and a wider readership. Jeffers submitted this poem to a collection of poems on the subject of California edited by George Sterling, James Rorty, and Genevieve Taggard; and it was considered such a fine piece by the editors that they chose to use it as the title for the collection.[9] In this early work, Jeffers announces the kind of profoundly inhuman perspective that would structure and inform all his mature poetry. The poem begins with Jeffers addressing "mother earth" from the edge of the North American continent at his home in Carmel. He remarks on the earth's massive presence, sensing behind him "Mountain and plain, the immense breadth of the continent," and out in front of him "the mass and doubled stretch of water" (CP 1, 16; SP, 24). Reflecting on the emergence of human

---

8 The issue of the nature and extent of consciousness in Jeffers's work is a complex one. For further analysis, see: George Hart, *Inventing the Language to Tell It: Robinson Jeffers and the Biology of Consciousness* (New York: Fordham University Press, 2013); and Christopher Damien, "Robinson Jeffers and the Contemplation of Consciousness," in *The Wild That Attracts Us: New Critical Essays on Robinson Jeffers*, ed. ShaunAnne Tangney (Albuquerque, NM: University of New Mexico Press, 2015), 1–24.

9 Jeffers tells the story of how, after submitting "Continent's End" for this collection, he sent both Rorty and Sterling copies of his privately printed edition of *Tamar*, which Rorty reviewed and then sent to fellow poetry critic Mark van Doren, who published his own review. It was largely on the strength of these reviews, and the interest they generated, that Jeffers's work was eventually picked up by Boni and Liveright. See CL 3, 949–52.

beings and other life forms within their evolutionary context and their subsequent historical development, Jeffers again speaks to the earth: "You were much younger when we crawled out of the womb and lay in the sun's eye on the tideline. / It was long and long ago, we have grown proud since then and you have grown bitter" (CP 1, 16; SP, 24).

But rather than simply deepening his reflections on human evolution (as the reader is led to expect from the opening lines), Jeffers instead changes tack and decides to describe his own poetic work—or more precisely, the deep structure, impulse, and measure of that work—as deriving from a time *before* life evolved on earth. Still addressing mother earth, he states: "The tides are in our veins, we still mirror the stars, life is your child, but there is in me / Older and harder than life and more impartial, the eye that watched before there was an ocean" (CP 1, 16; SP, 24). This older, more inhuman, abiotic eye looked on, Jeffers tells us, as the earth gradually accumulated its water, observed as life slowly emerged and eventually gave rise to human beings. The deep time that orients this eye and that gives it its hard, impartial character has its origins in the tumult of the early, formative stages of the earth; as such, it views life and human life in particular as the impermanent, relatively exceptional modes of existence that they are. There is beauty in life and in human existence, to be sure, but it manifests itself differently when viewed from the perspective of an abiotic and inhuman eye that sees through the lens of deep time and broader cosmic cycles. Thus, the splendor and beauty of things toward which Jeffers's poetry orients us is anything but the facile sort of aesthetic beauty that comes from merely turning one's eyes toward a scenic landscape; to see the sort of beauty and wonder he has in mind requires a different sort of attention and disposition, one forged in the ancient "tides of fire" that preceded the emergence of life as we know it and participate in it on an everyday basis.

This aesthetic and subjective disposition is also forged through a confrontation with the earth's ending—which is to say, with a sharp awareness of the fact that, even though the earth will persist well beyond any imaginable future for human life, it will eventually face its own end. The earth, too, belongs to the Wheel of Fortune, to the destruction and reconstitution of particles (to use Lucretian language)—a fact given new confirmation and significance with cosmological research coming to light in Jeffers's own era. In a piece published in 1937 entitled "Nova," Jeffers reflects on the recent sighting of a nova (perhaps Nova Sagittarii, which was visible to the naked eye and spotted in 1936) that, he notes, was at one time a "moderate star like our good sun" but that "found a new manner of flaming ten-thousandfold / More brightly for a brief time" (CP 2, 530; SP, 520). The analogy made between the nova and our sun hints at our sun sharing the same ultimate fate. Although scientists of this era were not entirely sure of the life and death cycle of the sun, they assumed something of a similar ending for it. Jeffers speculates: "It is likely our moderate / Father the sun will sometime put off his nature for a similar glory" and the earth would share in that glory. He offers a poetic depiction—in equal parts beautiful and terrifying—of this likely "glory":

> [...] these tall
> Green trees would become a moment's torches and vanish, the oceans
>   would explode into invisible steam,
> The ships and the great whales fall through them like flaming meteors
>   into the emptied abysm, the six-mile
> Hollows of the Pacific sea-bed might smoke for a moment. Then the
>   earth would be like the pale proud moon,
> Nothing but vitrified sand and rock would be left on earth. This is a
>   probable death-passion
> For the sun's planets; we have no knowledge to assure us it may not
>   happen at any moment of time. (CP 2, 530; SP, 520)

Scientists today, of course, are more confident that the sun will burn brightly and safely for many billions of years more before exhausting the hydrogen in its core and beginning the cycle that will lead to its expansion and ultimate death. Regardless of the precise dates of this event, the "glory" and ultimate fate of the earth will remain the same. Astronomical precision about the eventual death of the sun is not, however, Jeffers's ultimate concern here. In the final lines of the poem, Jeffers recalls us to the more mundane fact that in the present moment the sun continues to shine "wisely and warm" and that life continues on its course. He thus brings us from other galaxies back down to the Milky Way, back down to earth, back down to the coastline in Carmel, back down to the young girls the poet sees bathing in the cold ocean. He remarks tenderly on their beauty and vitality: "they are beautiful animals, all life is beautiful" (CP 2, 530; SP, 520). It is precisely this intensified appreciation for life as such, life as it is lived here and now, that the poet ultimately has as his aim. Regardless of what happens to the sun in the relatively short or long term, we as living individuals "cannot be sure of [*this*] life for one moment" (CP 2, 530; SP, 520). The ultimate point of considering the life and death of stars, or the sun, or the earth is for Jeffers to reframe our own existence and to put it into proper perspective. He seeks to remind us that we, too, belong to these larger cosmic cycles of generation and destruction—and that the miracle of catching sight of the splendor of these recurring cycles can, if properly framed and appreciated, lead us to live and die more resolutely, more intensely, perhaps even more beautifully.

Here we see once again that the beauty and splendor of things, as Jeffers understands such phenomena, are not readily seen or grasped; seeing in a more inhuman manner requires both a sustained practice of contemplation as well as the grace of the world's coming to presence independent of human mastery. Jeffers speaks to this complex relation that produces beauty in "Evening Ebb" (CP 2, 4; SP, 298), where he relates how chance "rifts" in the "screen" of the world that occur in the cloudy, shadowy conditions at sunset one evening interrupt his normal vision and allow him to peer for a brief moment behind that phenomenal screen. What he catches sight of with these rifts (which are effectively no more than chance and subtle interruptions in his normal mode of all-too-human awareness and focus) is the *same* world but now manifesting itself as *another* world. This other world is a more-than-human world, an inhuman world carrying out its recurrent relations and persistent rhythms on its own, without us, with no concern for human affairs, a world rehearsing for "another audience" behind the scenes (the presumption being that, most of the time, human beings fail to constitute much of an audience, inasmuch as they are generally inattentive to the larger cycles in which things participate and unfold). It is here, in this other site—a site constituted through a combination of contemplation and chance encounters—that something of the strange splendor of things is glimpsed.

In the lyric "Oh Lovely Rock," Jeffers provides readers with a poignant description of this experience of catching sight of the beauty of things and how it sometimes arises in a mysterious, almost mystical flash. Here, Jeffers recounts taking an overnight hike with his son Garth and his son's friend and spending the night on a little gravel patch near Ventana Creek in the Santa Lucia Range. Garth recalls elsewhere that his father had a hard time sleeping under these conditions,[10] and Jeffers himself seems to confess as much in the poem, noting that he was still awake after midnight watching his son and his companion sleep. Jeffers revives the campfire they are using for warmth, which allows him better to see the faces of the boys and the massive gorge wall nearby. Even with the wall being composed of nothing but common diorite, and despite being "nothing strange," the poet's careful attention to the presence of the rock allows him to see it "as if […] for the first time" (CP 2, 546; SP, 529). Peering through the rift in the screen of his everyday world produced by the flickering of the firelight and his insomnia, the poet notes again that the rock wall was "nothing strange […] I cannot / Tell you how

---

10 Audry L. Lynch, *Garth Jeffers Recalls his Father, Robinson Jeffers: Recollections of a Poet's Son* (Lewiston, NY: Edwin Mellen Press, 2012), 6.

strange: the silent passion, the deep nobility and childlike loveliness: this fate going on / Outside our fates" (CP 2, 546; SP 529).

This shift in contemplative attention—from matters having to do with our own fates to that of the fate of the world beyond us—is what allows the all-too-familiar "stuff" of the nonhuman world around us to present itself otherwise, as fundamentally and genuinely inhuman. That rock wall, which would typically go unnoticed by most of us, was produced by the "tides of fire" that form the earth's ancient core; it long precedes and will likely long outlast the human affairs that occur in its presence, steadfastly remaining there in the mountain "like a grave smiling child" (CP 2, 546; SP, 529). As the poet returns his focus to the faces of the sleeping boys, he is struck by the fleetingness and finitude of human life: "I shall die, and my boys / Will live and die, our world will go on through its rapid agonies of change and discovery; this age will die," and yet this wall of rock will persist and continue to bear "the whole mountain above" (CP 2, 546–47; SP, 529–30).

The task of the poet here is to work patiently and recurrently to turn his and our attention outward and beyond ourselves to this more permanent fate going on outside our fates. In making this turn, we find something that could never disappoint us: the profound beauty of the inhuman world. The poet concludes "Oh Lovely Rock" by telling us that "I, many packed centuries ago, / Felt [the rock's] intense reality with love and wonder, this lonely rock" (CP 2, 547; SP, 530). In this way, the poet tells us that he has carried out his task—which is to find and behold with wonder the beauty of things, to "see into the life of things" (as Wordsworth would have it)—to the best of his abilities. But with the adjective "lonely," he seems to indicate that he is waiting for others to join him, for it is perhaps not just the rock out in the wilderness and away from people that is lonely; it might also be the case that the poet, too, who assumes an inhuman perspective and who tries to live and love things in an inhuman way, is profoundly devoid of human company, even when family and friends are nearby.

Beholding Truth

As we have seen thus far in this chapter, Jeffers follows his predecessor Lucretius in employing a materialistic and cosmic perspective to recall us to what are fundamentally existential matters. By reorienting us away from an all-too-human perspective and toward a more inhuman, cosmic perspective, these poets place human existence in a new frame. With human beings no longer occupying the center of either the earth or the cosmos as a whole, the possibility emerges of learning to see anew the beauty and splendor of the inhuman world; concomitantly, the opportunity also arises to learn to see ourselves as ancillary outgrowths of this world and to move beyond the anti-nature, anti-cosmic sentiments that animate much of civilized existence. In brief, in allowing an inhuman and cosmic perspective to inform our attention and structure our disposition, we enter into a new realm of potentials for seeing and living differently, for becoming something other than who we have been formed to be by the dominant culture.

The aim of Chapters 4 and 5 is to explore in more detail this transformation in who we are, both at the level of subjectivity and of values. But before turning to that task, more needs to be said about Jeffers's adoption of a cosmic and deep-time perspective in his poetry. For Jeffers, adopting such a perspective is not simply a matter of being fully modern or rigorously scientific; it is also essential for arriving at a new and enlarged conception of truth. Although a poet like Lucretius, who is writing in an ancient Roman context, is concerned with truth and epistemological questions more generally (Epicureanism has, of course, its own epistemological framework), for Jeffers issues concerning truth are crucial in new ways specific to our modern age.

The naturalist Rachel Carson spoke brilliantly to such contemporary concerns about truth in "The Real World Around Us," a 1954 address to an audience of women journalists.[11] The title of Carson's talk refers to the fact that modern human beings have increasingly cut themselves off from the more-than-human world and have sought to ensconce themselves in a "perilously artificial world" in ways that were both unthinkable and impossible for ancient peoples.[12] What Carson has in mind here is the way in which modern technology—she mentions housing developments built on razed land, freeways constructed on top of damned waterways, and power plants placed on protected lands—has substituted "man-made ugliness" for the beauties of the more-than-human world; and this has been done, she emphasizes, for the sake of little more than increased profits and materialistic lifestyles.[13]

For Carson, this sacrifice and destruction of the beauty of the "real" world is clearly an aesthetic matter; but it is also a matter of *truth* in a profound sense of the term. She quotes a line from the nature writer Richard Jeffries to illustrate this connection: "The exceeding beauty of the earth, in her splendor of life, yields a new thought with every petal."[14] Carson worries that our basic awareness of the human independence and beauty of the real world around us

---

11 Rachel Carson, "The Real World Around Us," in *Lost Woods: The Discovered Writing of Rachel Carson*, ed. Linda Lear (Boston: Beacon Press, 1998), 147–63.
12 Carson, "The Real World Around Us," 161.
13 Carson, "The Real World Around Us."
14 Carson, "The Real World Around Us," 162. The quotation is from Richard Jeffries, "The Pageant of Summer," *Eclectic Magazine* 38, no. 2 (1883): 145–54, quotation at 154.

is gradually being lost in contemporary technological societies; and with this ongoing loss of a sustained connection to the real world, we are concomitantly losing the *provocation* to think—which is to say, to be moved by realities that exceed us and to which we are forced to grow and respond should we wish to know them. The further we retreat into an "artificial world of [our] own creation," the more we insulate ourselves "with steel and concrete, from the realities of earth and water," the more careless and destructive we become, and the more we lose the gentleness and suppleness required for responsive, meditative thinking.[15]

It is against the modern intensification and spread of this highly mediated, buffered, and technologized form of life that Jeffers also develops his thinking on truth. Jeffers's primary critical target on this issue is what philosophers refer to as an *idealist* epistemology. In the simplest terms, idealism is the notion that truth and reality are to be found on the side of human cognition, and that what renders something true is ultimately dependent upon our (human) perception of it. This position is commonly associated with the bishop and philosopher George Berkeley, whose last name might recall us to Jeffers's character Rev. Dr. Barclay from the early narrative *The Women at Point Sur*. (Berkeley and Barclay not only share similar sounding last names, of course, but also certain epistemological commitments that Jeffers takes up critically in that narrative poem.) For Jeffers, not only are idealist notions about truth and reality wrongheaded; if they are maintained and practiced in the context of the modern technological era in which we live, they are disastrous. Jeffers warns that only "darkness" (CP 4, 534) awaits those who take up the idealist path, by which he means the dead-end of becoming further entrenched in our own minds and more entangled in the anthropocentric nets from which we need to free ourselves. To insist that truth resides in our own mind or is somehow essentially linked or reducible to us is to risk being further cut off from the inhuman forces and provocations that make responsive thinking and flourishing possible.

Jeffers suggests that nearly all the great human quests for truth suffer from similar forms of idealist limitations and anthropocentric darkness. In "Theory of Truth" he postulates that the search for truth reflects a kind of glitch or malfunctioning in human life, one that arises out of frustration with the conditions of our existence and a general lack of animal happiness. Echoing themes we examined in Chapter 2, Jeffers makes the case that the

---

15 For more on the notion of meditative (as opposed to calculative) thinking, see Martin Heidegger, "Memorial Address," in *Discourse on Thinking*, trans. John M. Anderson and E. Hans Freund (New York: Harper & Row, 1966), 43–57.

notions of truth that undergird the major world religions and philosophies—here he has in mind Taoism, Christianity, and Buddhism—are consistently stained by "aching strands of insanity" (CP 2, 608; SP, 547) that plague their founders. Unable to accept the hardships of existence and the general human discontent they see around them, these leaders construct images of the "real" world and of "true" humanity that lead us to turn further inward upon ourselves and to search for truth within an inter- and intra-human frame.

The conclusion that might be drawn from Jeffers's reflections on truth is that, given these repeated and near-universal human shortcomings, our search for truth and for meaning in life is in principle "foredoomed and frustrate" (CP 2, 610; SP, 549). But this conclusion would be premature, for, as Jeffers maintains, the problem is not with the search for truth per se but rather with the underlying passions that have traditionally animated this quest. The reason that idealism and most classical approaches to truth lead further into darkness is because they start from an anthropocentric locus and never leave its orbit. The way beyond this limit, Jeffers believes, is to orient ourselves toward and to be led by the "one light [that] is left us" (CP 3, 403; SP, 679), namely, the light and the beauty of the inhuman world. It is in this inhuman register of existence that truth—both epistemological and existential—is to be disclosed.

In order to follow Jeffers's thinking on this point, though, we have to be especially careful in how we understand such a process of disclosure (or revelation, as the case might be). It would be a mistake to think that Jeffers is offering a naïve realism (that is, an account of truth that suggests human beings have direct and unmediated access to the truth of inhuman realities that are independent of our minds) in place of the foredoomed notions of truth he is criticizing. To the contrary, Jeffers maintains that human knowledge is fundamentally mediated and subjective, that what happens in our minds and in our "bone vaults" is not simply isomorphic with the mind-independent realities that give rise to our thoughts and cognition. On this point, Jeffers shares the modesty about human epistemological achievements commonly associated with Immanuel Kant, who argues that human beings carry with them cognitive apparatuses that filter and organize reality in such a way as to make mediation unavoidable. There is no possibility, on Kant's or Jeffers's account, of stepping completely outside of a human perspective on the world in order to grasp it in its pure, unmediated, "noumenal" state.

Yet, this properly chastened and humble epistemological stance (which Kant calls transcendental idealism) does not, on Jeffers's analysis, do full justice to our complicated relation to the inhuman world. For Jeffers, the human condition is not simply one of being limited by an unavoidably anthropocentric perspective, inasmuch as inhuman realities have *their own* ways of getting around, behind, and through our mediating structures. This is a very different claim from that of the naïve realist who believes we can, by an act of our own will, slough off the mediating aspects of our perceptual and cognitive apparatuses in order to grasp the full truth of reality for ourselves. For Jeffers, inhuman realities come *to us* of their own accord; and they arrive not in clear and distinct forms but in revelatory "shocks and flashes" (CP 1, 239; SP, 147), as interruptive and disruptive intrusions into our consciousnesses and lives that remind us that the inhuman world is more-than-human, that it exceeds and precedes us, envelops and outstrips us, in myriad ways.

Thus, Jeffers proposes with his poetry what we might call a critical or modest realism, an account of truth and knowledge that maintains we are in contact with the real and that we can even come to know it (albeit only partially and incompletely) thanks to the intrusive "grace" of the inhuman world. But, as with Jeffers's interest in cosmology, the stakes of these epistemological and ontological considerations are to be found primarily in their implications for how we live our lives. It is at this intersection of the true and the good that we encounter Jeffers's conviction that life and experience are, contra pessimism, worth the trouble. In other words, his work suggests that, if we are in fact capable of knowing the world more or less completely, then we *should* live in such a way that we do come to know it as completely as possible—or, as he puts it in an unpublished 1949 poem, we ought to try to "dream" the world "whole" (CP 4, 534). In endeavoring to dream the world as wholly and fully as possible, we would in effect be seeking to gain as many different perspectives on reality as possible (an epistemological approach that philosophers call *perspectivalism*), and to allow reality to transform our sense of self and how we live. Such perspectives cannot be gained, Jeffers insists, by the sedentary reflections of the armchair philosopher or the professional poet trapped in their respective studies. Nor are they to be achieved simply by being familiar with the latest discoveries by cosmologists and other scientists. While Jeffers certainly gives science its due regard in this vein, as we have seen, he does not take the human dream of the whole to be coincident simply with the expansion of scientific knowledge. Truth of the sort Jeffers is most interested in is *existential* in nature. Varied perspectives on reality can only be achieved by living and experiencing them.

This is why Jeffers argues that we can dream the whole only by treating our life as an experiment in truth, as an active seeking out of experiences that would have us risk leaving ourselves in order to touch and be touched by inhuman realities. Thus, even though the practices of poetry and critical reflection might tempt us to orient ourselves primarily in the direction of conceptual refinement, intellectual abstraction, and the ideal of achieving spiritual wisdom, it should rather lead us through and beyond thought and language, through and beyond our "dreams," to a more profound and more open experience of the realities that constantly interrupt and provoke us. In "Return," Jeffers describes this kind of movement through and beyond language and poetry, reminding himself that as of late he has been "a little too abstract, a little too wise," and that it "is time [...] to kiss the earth again." He tells us of his plan to "go down to the lovely Sur Rivers / And dip my arms in them up to the shoulders" (CP 2, 409; SP, 499). The ultimate aim of such actions, he emphasizes, is not to collect more material for his poetry. The plan, rather, is to "touch things and things and no more thoughts" (CP 2, 409; SP, 499), inasmuch as the latter tend to block experience and trap us even further in the machinations of the all-too-human bone vault. Again, there is no naïve realism here, no unmediated contact with the truth of the real, but rather a desire to put oneself in the way of life's interruptions and provocations and to stay with them—or, as Jeffers in his later years reminds himself: "to take what comes: not to withdraw from any experience / An old man finds" (CP 4, 535).

Inhuman Virtues

In a late poem entitled "De Rerum Virtute," Jeffers returns to the theme of the search for truth in view of how this quest might function to reframe the place of human beings in the cosmos; and he does so in a way that would seem to complicate the reading I have offered thus far concerning his epistemological ideas about cosmic perspective and truth. The title of the poem is clearly meant to recall us to Lucretius's master work, *De rerum natura*. But rather than discoursing on the nature (*natura*) of things, Jeffers here reflects on their excellence or virtue (*virtus*).[16] The poem opens abruptly with a strolling narrator encountering the skull of a human being, which leads to consideration of the thoughts and emotions that have passed under this "bone vault," including the "curious desire of knowing / Values and purpose and the causes of things." The narrator suggests, rather pessimistically, that this person "never discovered much, / And now all's empty, a bone bubble, a blown-out eggshell" (CP 3, 401; SP, 677).

This pessimism about the human capacity for discovering truth and wisdom continues in the fourth stanza, where the narrator finds himself standing

---

16 The Latin term *virtus* carries many senses. When applied to nonhuman entities, it typically denotes their goodness, high value, strength, and so on. Thus, with the titular phrase *De rerum virtute*, Jeffers's emphasis on *virtus* might be read as his particular way of naming and characterizing the nature of things.

on a cliff at Soberanes Creek overlooking the magnificent Pacific Ocean and reflecting on the ongoing Korean War, a "bitter futile" war that stands in sharp contrast to the *virtus* of the more-than-human things surrounding him. The narrator suggests that this war is "too hot in mind" at the time for anyone to grasp any beauty in it. He goes on to state, in a series of lines that when read quickly might smack of simple misanthropy, that "it is hard to see beauty / In any of the acts of man: but that means the acts of a sick microbe / On a satellite of a dust-grain twirled in a whirlwind / In a world of stars [...]" (CP 3, 402; SP, 678). Pulling back from the possible misanthropic implications of these lines, the poet suggests that maybe something will come of these human beings in the future; regardless of their ultimate outcome, in the cosmic scheme of things, he believes they will not last long.

At this point, Jeffers inserts himself directly into the poem, announcing his entry with an em-dash and telling us that he is "short of patience" since his wife died, and that the hateful and spiteful wars he has lived through over the decades have gotten under his skin and affected him "to the bone" (CP 3, 402; SP, 678). Although Jeffers's critical language about human beings is particularly sharp here, we should not dismiss it simply as the by-product of depression over his wife's death or simple life-weariness. Rather, as part of his commitment to *parrēsia* in his poetry, to speaking frankly to his readers and avoiding flattering them, Jeffers believes he must share his struggle with the reader of trying to make full sense of the human condition, and with trying to fit human actions—and, more specifically, the horrors of human war and violence—into the broader beauty of things.

The fifth and final stanza of the poem would seem to suggest that we do *not* fit, that human beings do not reflect the *virtus* of things. The narrator (or, rather, Jeffers himself, for the line separating poetic persona and biographical person has been deliberately crossed here) suggests that only "One thing is left us" at this point in time: "the beauty of things not men; / The immense beauty of the world, not the human world" (CP 3, 403; SP, 679). Jeffers then abruptly suggests that we should try to get beyond the human perspective, to look directly "without imagination, desire, nor dream" at the mountains and the sea, the wonders of the earth and its creatures. Are they not beautiful?, he twice asks us. Are they not exemplars of *virtus*? "The beauty of things," he tells us "means virtue and value in them" (CP 3: 403; SP: 679). And it would seem, contrary to what his earlier poems had suggested about the irreducibility of mediation in human cognition, that we can intuit them directly, simply by looking and without relying on our all-too-human imaginations, desires, and dreams.

The poem ends, though, by undercutting this naïve realist gesture. An interlocutor asks the poet: Isn't this *virtus* to which the poet directs us in the "beholder's eye, not the world?" (CP 3, 403; SP, 679). Reversing course to the more familiar position we have outlined above, Jeffers replies: Certainly; what we see is undoubtedly a "translation" of the nature of things. But—and this is key for Jeffers—our human translation is provoked and engendered by a more-than-human reality beyond it, by the "transhuman / Intrinsic glory" (CP 3, 403; SP, 679) of things. The indubitable and independent glory of the transhuman and inhuman world assures us, Jeffers states, that "the world is sound" (CP 3, 403; SP, 679).

But what about human beings? Are we also sound? Are we also part of the intrinsic glory? The apparent misanthropy of "De rerum virtute" does not lift or evaporate in the final stanza. Rather, the poem ends on a paradoxical note, stating that human beings are in fact "a part" of the beauty and glory of things, but not in the same way that the sea lion, gull, hawk, desert landscape, or rain forest are a part. Jeffers refuses, again, to flatter us here. To be sure, we belong to the larger planetary scheme of things—we are not aliens, after all. But we are still described in the final lines of the poem as "the sick microbe" (CP 3, 403; SP, 679), and we would seem to belong to the world only in the sense that illness belongs to and is intrinsic to life. Should we take this apparently pessimistic and misanthropic stance for Jeffers's final word on human beings? Might there be another way in which to be human? Or, to what might amount to another way of saying the same thing, is there some way for us *not* to be human?

Chapter 4

HUMAN

The Tragedy of Humanism

In his poetry and letters, Jeffers both laments and appreciatively acknowledges the highly rigorous education he received under the direction of his father. As I noted in the Introduction, this intensive education began with Jeffers literally having Latin slapped into him by his father in early childhood and continued into his youth and teen years during which he attended a series of demanding European schools (where classes were taught in foreign languages that Jeffers had to learn on the fly). By the time Jeffers had completed his education, he had a solid command of Greek, Latin, French, and German and had read widely in classical literature. Despite the downsides of this demanding program (the most obvious being his abbreviated childhood [CL 2, 1018]), his thorough training in classical languages and literatures left Jeffers with a profound and lasting appreciation for classical Greek poetry and epic; and he regularly draws inspiration and plots for his own poetry from these ancient narrative wells. Greek tragedy plays an especially prominent role in his *oeuvre*, with plays from Euripides and Aeschylus providing the backbone for some of his longer narratives.[1] Over the course of his career, Jeffers also composed several adaptations of ancient Greek tragedies.[2] These reworkings are no mere translations or paraphrases on Jeffers's part, but are instead original retellings tailored to explore a theme central to his own poetry while also speaking to the perennial issues highlighted by the original text.

---

1 Among these works, see especially: "Cawdor" (CP 1, 409–521; SP, 182–294), which includes several leitmotifs from Euripides's *Hippolytus*; and "Solstice" (CP 2, 487–512), which alludes to key themes in Euripides's *Medea*.
2 See, for example: "The Tower Beyond Tragedy" (CP 1, 119–78; excerpt in SP, 112–14) based on Aeschylus's *Oresteia*; "Medea" (CP 3, 139–97), based on Euripides's *Medea*; and "The Cretan Woman" (CP 3, 315–63), which is based on Euripides's *Hippolytus*.

Although Jeffers's general relationship to ancient Greek poetry has been ably explored by scholars in both Jeffers studies and in classics,[3] some of his reworkings of ancient Greek tragedies and themes have received less attention than others. One important piece by Jeffers that has received only minimal attention to date, "The Humanist's Tragedy," and which was published in his collection *Cawdor* (1928), will form my focus in the initial portion of the present chapter. This narrative is a brief retelling of a few key episodes in Euripides's posthumously produced and historically influential tragedy *Bacchae*.

Euripides's original play opens with a monologue by Dionysus who explains that he is traveling to Thebes to announce his divinity, where his divine status has been flatly denied by King Pentheus and his mother Agave and Agave's sisters. Dionysus first induces a frenzy in the women and sends them into the woods on Mount Cithaeron, then turns his attention to undermining Pentheus's skepticism. Pentheus, despite pleadings and admonitions from the elders Cadmus (his grandfather) and Tiresias (the blind prophet) to join in the Dionysian rites, stubbornly refuses the legitimacy of the new religion, convinced that its followers simply use it as a pretext to engage in debauchery. Dionysus, disguised as a visiting stranger and votary promulgating the new religion, is arrested, put in shackles, and imprisoned by Pentheus.

At this point in the story, Dionysus begins to demonstrate explicit signs of his divinity and causes an earthquake to topple Pentheus's palace. A messenger then arrives to tell Pentheus of the miraculous things the women on Mount Cithaeron are doing, including releasing water springs from rocks, nursing wild animals, tearing apart live cattle with their bare hands, and defeating male soldiers from a nearby village in a battle. Believing that the women might be involved in seedier behavior, Pentheus is easily induced by Dionysus to travel to the woods to spy on the women. Dionysus suggests that Pentheus will be less identifiable if he disguises himself as a woman, to which Pentheus agrees. Once they arrive in the woods, Pentheus watches the women in hiding from the top of a fir tree, but is spotted by the women and mistaken (due to their being in a trance) for a young mountain lion. They tear the tree down, making Pentheus fall to the ground, then tear his body into pieces and scatter it. Pentheus's mother Agave, still in a trance and still believing she has killed a mountain lion, stakes Pentheus's severed head on her wand and triumphantly marches into Thebes. Cadmus gathers the scattered body parts of

---

3 There are too many such sources to list here, but exemplary pieces of scholarship along these lines include: Mark Griffith, "Robinson Jeffers and Greek Tragedy," *Jeffers Studies* 7, no. 1 (Spring 2003): 19–50; and Edmund Richardson, "Re-living the Apocalypse: Robinson Jeffers's *Medea*," *International Journal of the Classical Tradition* 11 (2005): 369–382.

his grandson and then gently helps to bring Agave out of her trance and face the truth of what she has done. The play ends with Dionysus announcing that Thebes must suffer because of the actions of Pentheus and that Cadmus and his family are to be sent into exile.

In Jeffers's retelling of *Bacchae*, Pentheus's tragedy is the tragedy of a humanist—which is to say, it is the tragedy of someone who believes in and seeks to maintain human identity and uphold human supremacy against forces that threaten to annul that project. For Jeffers's Pentheus, it is the Dionysian religion (with its connotations of animal passion, drunkenness, sexual excess, and Bacchic revelry) that poses just such a threat. In opposition to the slackening of propriety that Dionysian energies bring in their wake, Pentheus defines himself in Jeffers's version of the play as a "human being, a king and a Greek," "mindful of all his dignity," different in kind from a "beast borne on the flood of passion" or a "boat without oars" (CP 1, 379). Upon the arrival of a votary (Dionysus disguised), Pentheus orders a messenger to take the man out of town. But when the messenger returns, he tells Pentheus that the stranger could not hear his orders and would only address the women on the mountain; he also reluctantly tells Pentheus that his mother Agave is involved in the Dionysian rituals. Distraught but "housing his wrath in hard self-mastery" (CP 1, 380), Pentheus travels to the mountain to investigate.

When he arrives, Pentheus finds the women half-naked and singing, wine and sweat dripping from their bodies. "Fools," he thinks to himself, these women who have lost all their dignity and forgotten the human pride of being "the only self-commanding animal, / That captains his own soul and controls even / Fate, for a space" (CP 1, 380). But for all his confidence in human distinction and dignity, Jeffers's Pentheus is still prone to a certain amount of doubt, even pessimism, about this propriety. Continuing his reflections on human uniqueness, he determines that human beings are also unique in their ability to employ instrumental rationality. But, he wonders, what, precisely, are the ends that most human beings pursue with their rational plans? Pentheus concludes that most of what human beings do in their daily lives tends toward trivial ends: comfort, satiation, and security. Spitting on the earth in disgust, Pentheus ponders whether the human condition really amounts to anything more than a fruitless and meaningless search for the basest sorts of pleasure.

Turning his ear to the women, Pentheus hears them speaking mysteriously about an "opening" they have found, a "wild strait gate-way" (which the reader later learns might be a path leading outside the orbit of interhuman affairs), but he is unable to understand their "madness" (CP 1, 381). He then pulls back his attention from the women's talk and returns to his reflections on the human condition. "Recollecting" his dignity that has been temporarily fragmented (mirroring the dismemberment his body will soon suffer), he suddenly recalls the "end" or aim of human existence: "The generations [...] aspire. / They better; they climb; as I / Am better than this weak suggestible woman my mother [...]. To increase the power, collectedness and dignity of man.—A more collected and dignified / Creature" (CP 1, 381). Pentheus's triumphant recollection of the noble ideals of the human is once again accompanied by a sour and pessimistic note, though, when he recalls that human beings, despite whatever dignity they might assume and achieve, share the same fate as the other animals: "to die and stink" (CP 1, 381).

At this juncture of the narrative, Dionysus himself walks into the midst of the women and offers them gentle words on how to live and die well and how to engage with and participate in the beauty of things. I will return to this speech in Chapter 5. For the moment, we need only note that Pentheus, the good humanist, characteristically ignores the speech and continues to see Dionysus as his enemy. Pentheus angrily goes in among the women to fetch his mother and reconstitute kingly order, but ends up suffering the same fate as Euripides's Pentheus: he is torn to pieces and his mother carries his head back down to Thebes, believing in her trance state that her son's head is that of a lion.

The Anthropological Machine

Jeffers's focused rewriting of these key scenes from the *Bacchae* constitutes one of his most succinct attempts to outline the futility of the presuppositions and ultimate aims of the humanist project. The humanist's overarching concerns, as "The Humanist's Tragedy" exhibits them, are to maintain: human distinctives (Pentheus as a *human being* rather than a beast); power (Pentheus as *king*); masculinity (Pentheus as a *man* and opposed to the effeminacy of Dionysus and his female worshippers); rank (Pentheus as *dignified*); and national and ethnic identity (Pentheus as the *Greek* who repels barbarian outsiders). In Jeffers's narrative, Pentheus's defiantly humanist stance is tragic because he fails to see that finding the path to living and dying well, to seeing and engaging with the beauty of things, requires us fundamentally to take leave of this project and to go beyond the task of maintaining human distinctives and propriety. Leaving behind this project would require us to dismantle and turn our backs on what Giorgio Agamben calls the *anthropological machine*,[4] the conceptual and institutional structures that recurrently define human propriety

---

4 Giorgio Agamben, *The Open: Man and Animal*, trans. Kevin Attell (Stanford: Stanford University Press, 2004).

over and against human animality, other-than-human animals, and the rest of the more-than-human world. But even if we might acquiesce to the idea that humanism of Pentheus's sort is a bankrupt and futile project, the question might still be raised: How can those of us who have been trained for so long now to be good humanists and "practical people" (CP 1, 112)—oriented as we are by interhuman circuits of communication and instrumental rationality—stop the anthropological machine and leap into the non-teleological comedy of life and its beauty? How can we human beings be anything other than human?

Across the course of his career, Jeffers's poetry attempts to chart a path beyond the orbit of humanism and anthropocentrism in various ways, and my aim in the rest of this chapter is to assemble the key insights of those different efforts into a coherent framework that I hope illuminates the stakes and promise of this approach. As with the cosmically and epistemologically oriented poetry that I analyzed in the previous chapter, it is important to note here as well that Jeffers refuses to flatter human beings in diagnosing our condition. Indeed, his reflections on the emergence, evolution, and present-day existence of human beings—the human beings we must overcome if we wish to become something other and better than who we currently are—contain what appear to be profoundly misanthropic remarks. Yet, as I will argue, this unflattering and largely negative portrayal of human beings is not the simple misanthropy it appears to be at first glance. Rather, Jeffers's highly critical analysis of the human and the humanist project is part of a deliberate strategy intended to dislodge our standard views of who we are and constitutes an essential component in his broader task of sketching another ideal for human beings, one in which we find ourselves by losing ourselves.

The Human Dawn

By contrast with the humanist project which posits that human beings have a purpose and larger aim on earth they are designed to pursue and fulfill, Jeffers's medico-scientific training leaves him with a fundamentally non-anthropocentric and non-teleological conception of the human condition.[5]

---

5 Jeffers explains the relation between his childhood education and his more advanced education and medical training in a letter to Hyatt Howe Waggoner: "My father was a clergyman but also intelligent, and he brought me up to timely ideas about origin of species, descent of man, astronomy, geology, etc., so that progress was gradual, none of the view-points of modern science came as a revelation. Studies in university and medical school gave me more room to move in, more points of support, but never, that I remember, any sudden readjustment" (CL 2, 770).

Much like Charles Darwin (1809–82), who is a constant presence in Jeffers's work despite only being mentioned by name in the narrative poem "The Inhumanist," Jeffers refuses to grant human beings a separate or special status in the natural scheme of things. For Jeffers, we belong entirely to this world, and our emergence and present condition are to be understood in entirely naturalistic terms. While Darwin's *Origin of Species* (1859) hinted at this naturalistic approach to human evolution and *The Descent of Man* (1871) explicitly sketched out the path human evolution might have taken, Darwin himself lacked sufficient empirical evidence to settle the issue of human descent by modification in a convincing way. By the time Jeffers reached the mature phase of his poetry in the 1920s, however, such evidence had multiplied considerably, and his poetry consistently reflects these scientific advances.

Several of Jeffers's poems speculate on the forces and conditions underlying human evolution, among the most memorable being his "Original Sin." Here Jeffers rewrites the Edenic and Promethean myths of human origins using a naturalistic frame. He describes ancient hunters who have dug a pitfall and captured a mammoth with it, trying to get at "the life in [its] hide" (CP 3, 203; SP, 585) and to turn that life into consumable meat. With only flint weapons at their disposal, the hunters try in vain to get at the mammoth's flesh. Suddenly, one of the hunters remembers the fire they are using to guard their cave and goes to fetch it. The hunters build a fire and burn the mammoth alive, gleefully watching the "long hairy trunk / Waver over the stifle trumpeting pain" (CP 3, 203; SP, 585). Reminiscent of the opening stanza of "Apology for Bad Dreams" (see Chapter 1), Jeffers places this primal scene of cruelty and violence against the backdrop of the beauty of the sunrise, the landscape, and the morning breeze. Standing in the midst of the overwhelming beauty of things but failing to attend to it, "hour after hour, the happy hunters / Roasted their living meat slowly to death." "These are the people," Jeffers tells us: "This is the human dawn" (CP 3, 203; SP, 585).

In an ambitious poem that Jeffers left untitled and unpublished at his death (CP 3, 430–34; SP, 689–93), he revisits the scene of human origins and tries to tell a more expansive story that places human evolution in a broader cosmic and planetary context. Once again mirroring Lucretius's *De rerum natura*, Jeffers's poem seeks to bring the entire sweep of the history of the earth and the emergence of human and nonhuman life into narrative form. Starting from the earth in its initial "unformed volcanic" (CP 3, 430; SP, 689) state, Jeffers describes the long process of life's formation, from gases to proteins to the first cells and on to individual organisms, plants, and animals. The story he relates here is intended to do more, though, than place scientific facts in narrative form; rather, Jeffers endeavors to inscribe a certain degree of life and consciousness into *all* of existence. In so doing, he is not defending vitalism against mechanism but is instead maintaining that the conscious awareness we commonly think of as a human distinctive is not exclusive to us (CL 2, 848–49). In line with Darwinian ontology, Jeffers insists that what occurs with the advent of human consciousness is not something different in kind from other forms of existence but something different only in degree. We human beings are perhaps distinctive to the degree that we "concentrate" consciousness and bring it into "focus" (CP 3, 432); but we do so not of our own volition or to reach our own self-determined *telos*. Rather, we do so as part of a much larger process of the universe as a whole (or God, or nature) becoming aware of itself and relating to itself in ever different forms.[6]

Lest the reader suspect that Jeffers is here smuggling in a classical theism and teleology that would undercut a materialist and evolutionary perspective on human beings, he again takes up the issue of human existence in a strongly naturalistic way. He makes a "guess" on our origins, pinning the transition to bipedalism on a "change of climate" that forced us down from the trees and onto the ground to secure new food sources (CP 3, 432; SP, 691).[7] He speculates that the prey animals we encountered there, though, made existence a "dream of death" for us, leading us to become defensive and frightened, and to kill out of "pure terror" (CP 3, 433; SP, 692). We were forced to stand upright and stay alert, constantly ready to fight. In Promethean fashion, we made weapons for ourselves and learned to use fire. With this posture and these defenses, Jeffers suggests, we managed to survive the "shock and agony" of this transition to life on the ground (CP 3, 433; SP, 692).

Jeffers's description of human beings turns decidedly negative at this juncture of his narrative, mirroring his account of the human dawn in "Original Sin." He describes newly emergent human beings as "cruel and bloody-handed" and sees our earlier experiences of terror as leaving their traces in the invention of human language and the stories we tell about ourselves to each other. None of our early epics and religious narratives, he reminds us,

---

6 Here, again, there are points of resonance in Jeffers's poetry with the pantheism (or panentheism) of philosophers like Spinoza and Hegel. Whether these philosophers are properly characterized as theists or atheists is outside the scope of my concern here; what is important for the purposes of the present discussion, though, is to stress that whether we call the whole of things "God" or "nature" or even "Chaos" (following Nietzsche, who also belongs to the orbit of this approach), it is an entirely *immanent* whole for Jeffers—and this whole does not point beyond itself to a transcendent, supernatural origin. For Jeffers's prose reflections on his notion of pantheism, see especially CP 4, 411–12.
7 Jeffers is alluding to the so-called "savannah hypothesis" about the origins of bipedalism, which has now generally fallen out of favor with scientific researchers.

unfold without "the blood-splash" at the center; all are "cruel and bloody" (CP 3, 433; SP, 692). In our better moments, we tell ourselves we are just a "little lower than the angels"; Jeffers responds by stating flatly that we are "blood-snuffing rats" (CP 3, 433; SP, 692).

These are, of course, not the only harsh sentiments regarding humanity expressed in Jeffers's poetry. We have already encountered similar remarks in our reading of "De rerum virtute" at the end of the previous chapter; and these sorts of statements recur with troubling regularity across his corpus—and, in his late poetry, with increasing frequency. To take up one striking example, consider the late poem "Orca" (first published in 1947), which recounts Jeffers's experience of seeing orcas killing sea-lions just offshore from his overlook. In this piece, Jeffers does not downplay the panic or sad fate of the sea lions but openly acknowledges their terror and death at the hands of the whales. But the killing he witnessed among the animals, he writes, "looked clean and bright, it was beautiful" (CP 3, 206; SP, 588). Deadly animal-animal interactions of this sort stand in sharp contrast to the deceit and cruelty that saturate human wars (earlier in the poem, he analogizes the huge black bodies of the orcas with the "flying vipers with which the Germans lashed London" [CP 3, 205; SP, 587]). Among animals, there are "no lies, no smirk and no malice; / All strict and decent" (CP 3, 206; SP, 588). With just this more-than-human world in mind, even with its stark violence on display, the earth looks like a shining star; but, Jeffers suggests, we human beings darken that star. We have been "queer from the start" and look like a "botched experiment" (CP 3, 206; SP, 588) that is out of control and should be stopped. There are dozens of similarly harsh remarks in Jeffers's work, where human beings are analogized with filth to be washed away, and described as ridiculous, atrociously ugly, wretched, farcical, and so on.[8] One can thus hardly fault the critic who concludes that his poetry preaches disgust of human beings. Jeffers not only tempts the reader in this interpretive direction, he actively encourages it.[9]

---

8 For representative examples, see: "November Surf" (CP 2, 159; SP, 381); "Still the Mind Smiles" (CP 2, 310; SP, 399); "The Answer" (CP 2, 536; SP, 522); and "The Beautiful Captive" (CP 3, 428–29).

9 See "Crumbs or the Loaf" (CP 2, 381), where Jeffers recognizes that readers who understand and believe what his poetry has "clearly seen," will likely conclude that he hates humankind and tries to annihilate meaning in our lives. Jeffers contests this conclusion in several places, of course, but he clearly anticipates being read in this manner.

The Great Frame

As Nietzsche wisely notes, though, "one pays too dearly for hatred of man."[10] Indeed, one pays twice for misanthropy when viewed from the coordinates that structure Jeffers's larger philosophical-poetical framework. On the one hand, a misanthropy that is grounded in a difference in kind between the human and more-than-human worlds leads to an ontological dead-end in which human beings appear to be ontological aliens, imported from another planet or dropped off here by supernatural means. On the other hand, if it is granted that human beings do in fact belong entirely to the natural world but our actions are described in largely misanthropic and pessimistic terms, then finding a place for the wide variety of human actions and dispositions in the larger beauty and wonder of things is a challenge; here, too, on the aesthetic register we still appear to be an inexplicable exception to the general *virtus* of things.

How, then, does Jeffers stand in regard to the human? Does his work amount to nothing more than a radical rejection of human existence in favor of nonhuman nature and undisturbed wilderness? Is the philosophy guiding his poetry just garden-variety misanthropy and pessimism writ large? I believe something subtler is going on in Jeffers's work and that he understands all too well the price to be paid for misanthropy and for adopting a pessimistic view of the human condition.[11] In regard to the first (ontological) horn of the dilemma we have just raised, Jeffers ultimately refuses to separate human beings from the rest of existence (despite certain passages that might suggest otherwise). On an ontological register, it is clear that Jeffers is a *monist* (the position that there is but one substance or basic sort of stuff in the world, that this substance gets differentially distributed, and that such differences should be understood in terms of degree rather than kind).[12] In "Monument" (CP 3, 419), for example, Jeffers pleads with the reader to "erase the lines" created by classificatory schemas and to recognize that "the thing is like a river, from source to sea-mouth / One flowing life. We […] / Are one flesh with the beasts, and the beasts with the plants / One streaming sap, and certainly the plants and algae and the earth they spring from, / Are one flesh with the stars." In this vein, he endeavors throughout his work to present all beings

---

10 Friedrich Nietzsche, *The Gay Science: With a Prelude in Rhymes and an Appendix of Songs*, trans. Walter Kaufmann (New York: Vintage Books, 1974), 341.
11 See Jeffers's rejection of misanthropy in "The Dreaming River" (CP 4, 528), where he refers to it as madness and counsels balancing and neutralizing this "unclean" emotion.
12 Jeffers outlines his monistic commitments in a letter to Frederic Carpenter (CL 2, 81).

and relations within the "great frame [that] takes all creatures" (CP 1, 118; SP, 111), human beings included. Whatever divisions and classifications that one finds in his work are thus to be understood as *memoria technica* (CP 3, 419), categories to be used as shorthand but never to be taken as a substitute for the dynamic, unified reality that underlies them.

Yet, even as Jeffers underscores this oneness provided by the great frame, and affirms that human beings belong to the same source as all other entities, he seems to accept this fact only begrudgingly. There is something about human beings that makes him almost seem to regret our collective existence, as well as his own belonging to the species. We have already seen Jeffers's comment in "Original Sin" indicating that he would rather be a worm in an apple than a human being. There is also Jeffers's famously inflammatory line in "Hurt Hawks" concerning how he would "sooner […] kill a man than a hawk" (CP 1, 377; SP, 165) when considering whether to euthanize an injured bird. Similarly, in "The Tower Beyond Tragedy," Cassandra voices her desire for a speedy metamorphosis into a nonhuman form upon death, a desire to have humanity cut out of her being, for "that is the wound that festers" (CP 1,149).

Some headway can be made in understanding the force and effect of Jeffers's critical attitude toward the human species if we bear in the mind the split between the *ontology* and *aesthetics* of our belonging to the whole. In ontological terms, as already noted, Jeffers has no intention of denying our belonging to the whole or of positing a different nature, substance, or origin to account for the human condition. He is unwaveringly committed to placing things within the capacious naturalism of a broad ontological perspective that accepts and makes room for everything, whether human or more-than-human. Acknowledging our ontological kinship with the whole of things does not, however, tell us how we *do* (in fact) and how we *might* otherwise (i.e., how we should or ought) relate to and interact with the *beauty* of things.

In terms of the former, factual aspects of human action and human history, Jeffers often struggles to understand how they fit into the larger scheme of things. As I suggested in Chapter 2, this issue is central to the secular version of the problem of evil. Much of our past and present is blood-soaked and colored by cruelty, as Jeffers frequently reminds us; and while we can find similar bloodshed and violence in the natural world, interhuman relations often exhibit these characteristics to an extraordinarily and alarmingly high degree. Jeffers believes we flatter ourselves when we suggest that cruelty resides primarily in nonhuman nature and that kindness and virtue are to be found only on the other side of that divide within human culture. He believes that part of his calling is to join the few poets and philosophers who proffer an honest account of our actions and to try, with intellectual probity, to fit our actions into a naturalistic schema.

Similarly, Jeffers has little interest in issuing *moral* condemnations of our actions. He maintains that our violent tendencies have deep roots in our evolutionary past, and that heaping moral blame on human beings for their actions is effectively pointless—not because we altogether lack agency but because much of our behavior occurs unconsciously and outside the scope of rational reflection.[13] Rather than being moral in nature, Jeffers's objections to much of human behavior and culture can be better understood as *ethico-aesthetic*. His criticisms of human beings imply that it is possible—and that it would be better—for us to live *differently* from and more *beautifully* than we typically do. Ethically speaking, the issue here is one of shame rather than blame: we should feel ashamed of our baser and uglier acts because we are capable of living more remarkably and more beautifully than we often do. Aesthetically speaking, we are being challenged to take up a different relation to the beauty of things. Jeffers is suggesting that not only could we learn to orient ourselves to the beauty of things more consistently and persistently, we might also, through sustained practice, learn to *add* to that beauty. To be sure, everything we do fits more or less into the beauty of things as a whole—but this "more or less" marks the difference between a beautiful life that is well lived as opposed to a life that simply feeds into the ongoing decline of contemporary culture. These points about the ethics and aesthetics of a life well lived will occupy us at more length in the following chapter. For the moment, however, it is necessary to examine the upshot of viewing humans within the perspective of this great frame.

How (Not) to Be Human

In challenging the humanist perspective and its inherent "tragedy," Jeffers implies the need to fundamentally transform both our sense of self and our place in the larger scheme of things. As we have seen, Jeffers maintains throughout his poetry that we are not utterly distinct from or more remarkable than the more-than-human world; what is more, he suggests that in our vain efforts to institute an anthropological difference, we have given massively outsized attention and value to human existence and interhuman affairs. Jeffers's poetry counters this anthropocentrism by recalling us to the fact that there are more-than-human beings just as worthy of our attention, and that there are inhuman temporalities, relations, and forces whose beauty and majesty we might come to appreciate. In directing ourselves outward

---

13 See CP 4, 433 and CP 3, 25/SP, 653. See also Frederic I. Carpenter, "Robinson Jeffers Today: Beyond Good and Beneath Evil," *American Literature* 49 (1977): 86–96.

beyond the traditional notion of the human and its concomitant tragedy, we make the first step toward becoming something other than human.

Another essential step on this transformative path is to appreciate the relative youth and transience of human existence. Given the brevity of the hominin lineage and the even more recent emergence of *Homo sapiens* (which scientists currently date to roughly 200,000 years ago), and given the grim prospects at present for the long-term survival of the species, there is little reason to puff ourselves up in terms of our biological importance. Jeffers emphasizes this perspective in several poems, anticipating the day when people will be "fewer and the hawks more numerous" ("November Surf," CP 2, 159; SP, 381), when we as individuals and as a species will be "supplanted" ("Hands," CP 2, 4; SP, 298), and when our "iron age" will pass and leave behind nothing but "stains of rust on mounds of plaster" and the occasional "thigh-bone" ("Summer Holiday," CP 1, 202). And after we are gone, the cycles of life and death will persist, just as they did long before we were here, and the "earth [will] flourish long after mankind is out" ("The End of the World," CP 3, 441).

This gesture of decentering and relativizing human beings is, of course, not entirely novel with Jeffers; there is a long tradition of similar non-anthropocentric thinking among both philosophers and poets.[14] And the more observant among these figures have recognized that simply marking human transience and smallness does not always lead to an affirmative transformation or betterment in the human condition. In fact, as Nietzsche (who is among the most trenchant critics of an inflated sense of human importance) remarks, the downgrading of human significance and decentering of human beings relative to broader cosmological and ontological realities might even have the unintended effect of intensifying our pessimism and nihilism about the value of human life. In *On the Genealogy of Morality*, he asks:

> Hasn't precisely the self-belittlement of man, his will to self-belittlement been marching relentlessly forward since Copernicus? Alas, the belief in his dignity, uniqueness, irreplaceability in the hierarchy of beings is lost—he has become an *animal*, without simile, qualification, or reservation an animal, he who in his earlier belief was almost god ("child of God," "God-man") [...] Since Copernicus man seems to have stumbled onto an inclined plane—he is now rolling faster and faster away from the center—whither? into nothingness? into the "*penetrating* feeling of his

---

14 For a helpful survey of this tradition, which also includes material on Jeffers, see Bryan L. Moore, *Ecological Literature and the Critique of Anthropocentrism* (Cham, Switzerland: Palgrave Macmillan, 2017).

nothingness?" [...] So be it! exactly this would be the straight path—into the *old* ideal?[15]

Some one hundred years before Nietzsche wrote those words, Immanuel Kant alluded to similar worries at the same time as he famously expressed his "ever new and increasing admiration and reverence" that filled him when he studied the "*starry heavens*" above him.[16] Kant knew full well that the vastness of those starry heavens situated him and other human beings within "an unbounded magnitude [of] worlds upon worlds," and that a properly cosmic perspective "annihilates [...] my importance as an *animal creature*, which [...] must give back to the planet (a mere speck in the universe) the matter from which it came."[17] As is well known, Kant recoiled from the full implications of what he glimpsed in the night sky. He created other perspectives and "faculties"—namely, those of practical reason and teleological judgment—from which to view human beings, perspectives that would preserve our dignity and pride of place within the natural order. This reactionary gesture is what leads Nietzsche to suggest elsewhere that even though Kant's radical commitment to explaining experience in scientific terms had broken open the cage of superstition that had previously held human beings in place, Kant ultimately leads us back into that same cage, like a fox that has lost its way and gone astray back into captivity.[18] The question that Nietzsche's thought poses for us is whether it is possible to go as far down the road of deflating human significance as we have done here with Jeffers and not end up either (1) intensifying pessimism and nihilism concerning the human condition (a position Nietzsche associates with contemporary secular humanism), or (2) losing our nerve and retreating back to the familiar coordinates of an outmoded religious and ethical worldview (in line with Kant).

How does Jeffers negotiate this dilemma? The full significance and novelty of his approach can best be appreciated by contrasting it with Kant's response. If Kant responded to the growing recognition of human insignificance by doubling down on the uniqueness and dignity of human beings, we might be tempted to think that the non-anthropocentric Jeffers takes the opposing route and simply allows human beings to descend further into complete

---

15 Friedrich Nietzsche, *On the Genealogy of Morality*, trans. Maudemarie Clark and Alan Swensen (Indianapolis, IN: Hackett, 1998), 112.
16 Immanuel Kant, *Critique of Practical Reason*, trans. Mary Gregor, rev. Andrews Reath (Cambridge: Cambridge University Press, 2015), 129.
17 Kant, *Critique of Practical Reason*, 129.
18 Friedrich Nietzsche, *The Gay Science: With a Prelude in Rhymes and an Appendix of Songs*, trans. Walter Kaufmann (New York: Vintage Books, 1974), 264.

*in*significance. As we have seen, many of Jeffers's remarks on the human species would suggest as much. Yet, there is another thread in his poetry that suggests a different strategy on his part for engaging with the human condition. Rather than retrieving human dignity or allowing it to collapse into utter meaninglessness and valueless-ness, Jeffers makes the radical suggestion that *we can become something other than human.* Human beings are not a separate and distinct set with an invariant essence but rather form a part of an unfolding, dynamic whole that bears innumerable potentials. Human beings are experiments in the making. In short, his work subtly suggests and seeks to show us that we do not have to be human; we can be born again, and in so doing, become something other than human.

Of course, Jeffers is not suggesting that we can jump across what Gilles Deleuze and Félix Guattari call "molar species." Becoming something other than human is not a matter of, say, a member of *Homo sapiens* growing wings and talons and becoming a member of *Buteo jamaicensis* (to name one of Jeffers's favorite birds); as I have just noted, full recognition and affirmation of our biological inheritance is essential to Jeffers's poetry. Instead, becoming something other than human refers to becoming something other than who we typically strive to be (something other than what Deleuze refers to as the "dogmatic image" of the human). It means challenging the specific *project* and particular way of being in the world we have sought to actualize, the project symbolized in King Pentheus's pursuit of the institution and maintenance of human propriety and dignity at all costs. Figuring out how (not) to be human, then, is a matter of moving beyond this project and subject position and learning how to become something other than who we are at present—and to do so in view of the myriad biological, cultural, planetary, and cosmic potentials that constitute the present. In the next chapter, I will consider the shifts in perspective and practice that Jeffers suggests are requisite for learning how to become something other than human.

On Anthropocen(e)trism

A popular story has emerged in recent years about our contemporary condition, one that begins with rather different premises from the ones we are highlighting in Jeffers's poetry. Whereas Jeffers's work, as I have just suggested, seeks to decenter human beings and challenges traditional notions of human dignity and propriety, this other story—the story of the Anthropocene—insists on a certain kind of human identity and places human beings back in the center of planetary affairs. Before proceeding further down Jeffers's inhumanist path, it will prove helpful to pause and consider whether the sort of radical non-anthropocentrism he advocates is still tenable in view of the contemporary claims made about the centrality and importance of human beings in the narrative concerning the Anthropocene.

As the standard telling of the story goes, the Anthropocene concept was initially coined by scientists Paul Crutzen and Eugene Stoermer to name the recent geological era in which human beings have become the main drivers of planetary change.[19] The origins of this era can be dated, they argue, to roughly two hundred years ago, when a variety of human activities began to have a noticeable and measurable influence on planetary systems. This starting point also coincides with the Industrial Revolution, a period that ushered in extensive economic and technological innovations. Among the measurable impacts that human beings have had on the planet during this period, the most consequential include exponential human population growth, coupled with increased resource use and urban sprawl; massive land surface changes due to development and agriculture; an exponential increase in the rate of species extinction; the use of more than half of the earth's accessible fresh water; and increased emissions of greenhouse gases that have contributed to global climate change. Other scientists and researchers argue that the beginning of the Anthropocene era should be dated to some 8,000–10,000 years ago, when large-scale agriculture and animal domestication began and human beings first markedly altered their natural environment.[20] Whatever historical marker is used, the Anthropocene hypothesis proposes that human beings have, in the more-or-less recent past, transformed the geology and ecology of the earth in an epochal manner.

Despite Jeffers living only into the 1960s, he was certainly aware of the early manifestations of many of the human impacts associated with the Anthropocene and the general ecological degradation engendered by contemporary capitalist and consumerist lifestyles. (It should be recalled, after all, that even on the shortest timeline, the Anthropocene names an era that is *at least* two hundred years old; and the effects of human social, economic, and technological impacts on planetary systems have certainly not gone unnoticed until just recently.) He knew of and commented on the possibility of large-scale climatic changes (CP 3, 476) as well as the negative consequences of a rapidly expanding human population (CP 4, 435; CP 4, 440). To a certain extent, then, Jeffers's thinking aligns with the general thrust of

---

19 Paul Crutzen and Eugene Stoermer, "The Anthropocene," *Global Change Newsletter* 41 (2000): 12–13.
20 William F. Ruddiman, "The Anthropogenic Greenhouse Era Began Thousands of Years Ago," *Climatic Change* 61 (2003): 261–93.

the Anthropocene framework and reinforces the notion that modern human societies carry a significant planetary impact and presence.

Yet, there is something about the notion of the Anthropocene that makes for an ill fit with the kind of radically non-anthropocentric perspective we have been explicating in Jeffers's poetry. Although he acknowledges the growing impact of human beings on their surrounding environments and the planet as a whole, Jeffers nevertheless consistently downplays the long-term importance and centrality of human beings in both planetary and cosmic terms. Thus, even as the discourse surrounding the Anthropocene seeks to place us back in the center of the present era and the recent historical past, it seems clear that the sort of radically non-anthropocentric perspective we have been developing in these pages entails a fundamental rejection of this re-centering gesture, and for several interrelated reasons.

First, inasmuch as the *anthrōpos* of the Anthropocene is understood to denote a biological set, it must be noted that not all members of the biological species *Homo sapiens* have played the same role in determining the direction or impact of collective social life during this period. Most of the ecological degradation associated with the Anthropocene is due not simply to increased human population per se but has resulted in large part from the economic activities and interests of a relatively small percentage of humanity. This has led some critics, not unreasonably, to re-badge our era with the label of *Capitalocene*, a name that underscores the fact that the rapid rise in ecological degradation over the past two centuries is inextricably linked to the rise and interests of the capitalist class (which constitutes only a small fraction of *Homo sapiens*) and thus cannot be considered an inevitable consequence of human existence as such.

Second, the notion of the Anthropocene tends to reinforce an image of humanity as a standalone species, as somehow different in kind from other species and as having brought about widespread ecological degradation entirely on its own. While we have seen that Jeffers flirts with this image of humanity as alien to and inherently destructive of nature, he ultimately suggests that as a matter of intellectual probity and ontological integrity it is necessary to work through and beyond this idea and ultimately to place human beings back within the larger planetary and cosmic scheme of things. In so doing, the traditional manner of drawing sharp ontological differences in kind between human beings and others falls away, and the differences that remain between human and more-than-human become differences of degree, differences that emerge through relations, natural variations, and variable experiences that are more complex and dynamic than traditional binary oppositions allow.

As a corollary to this de-constitution of ontological binaries, it is becoming increasingly clear that if we wish to come to grips with the sources and extent of current ecological crises, it will be necessary to rid ourselves of the notion that we are a standalone, static species that brings about degradation on our own. For we remain, despite certain pretensions to the contrary, utterly dependent for our continued existence on multispecies relations at micro- and macro-levels in countless registers. We are enmeshed entirely in the ontological warp and woof of the more-than-human world. Thus, any serious response to the crises with which we are faced would be impossible to implement and sustain without the co-persistence of myriad interrelations that enable any autonomy and agency we might be able to exercise. Part of addressing our present is thus owning up to, affirming, and becoming responsible for these multi-species relations rather than trying to distinguish ourselves from them in the manner that Anthropocene discourse risks doing.[21]

These objections to the Anthropocene concept are not intended, of course, to avoid placing blame or responsibility for the present state of affairs where it is due; the point, rather, is to reframe the crises of our present age in order to rethink the way we have positioned ourselves inside and outside them. There is, to be sure, merit in recognizing and assessing the severity and urgency of the varied forms of social and ecological decline "we" have engendered. But if human beings occupy the focus and center of that analysis, as is often the case in contemporary Anthropocene discourse, we will persist in viewing ourselves as managers of a planet filled with "resources" for our use.[22] And rather than seeking to affirm and deepen our connections with our planetary kin, our goal as managers of "nature" will be to stabilize living conditions so that we can establish security and places of refuge primarily for ourselves. If, however, we give up on the notion that our condition is somehow independent and separate from that of our more-than-human kin, we will recognize that such an approach to the Anthropocene is an illusion. The decline we are witnessing cannot, at this point, be simply halted or reversed, not even by the most enlightened of human managers (although, declining conditions can certainly be further accelerated). These desperate and fraught conditions must, rather, be acknowledged as those under which all of us now live and

---

21 Donna Haraway, *Staying with the Trouble: Making Kin in the Chthulucene* (Minneapolis: University of Minnesota Press, 2016).
22 Eileen Crist, "On the Poverty of Our Nomenclature," *Environmental Humanities* 3 (2013): 129–47.

die—fragile and vulnerable, exposed to the very best and the very worst, in common with our planetary kin.[23]

Jeffers's poetry regularly recalls us to these sorts of existential bonds we share with our planetary kin, and this is ultimately what renders his poetry so fundamentally at odds with the thrust of much Anthropocene discourse. For, whereas some advocates of the Anthropocene concept might be willing to acknowledge certain parts of what has been argued above, there are few who would likely follow Jeffers in asserting that the key to living and dying well under present conditions is to deepen our sense of kinship with the more-than-human world, and to turn our focus beyond ourselves to the fragility and beauty of more-than-human others. In support of Jeffers inhumanist turn, though, it should be noted that interhuman affairs alone, despite their ubiquitous effects, constitute an incredibly small slice of planetary reality (and an even smaller fraction of cosmic reality). To be sure, we can do great damage to the planet for whatever brief time we are ultimately here; but no matter the extent of our contribution (whether negative or positive), it will never merit the inflated sense of ourselves that we have been encouraged to adopt by our anthropocentric culture. Within and well beyond our lives and interhuman circuits of media and communication, there are countless other-than-human relations, beings, and transformations that unfold in all of their earnestness, beauty, and significance. If there is any salvation and consolation to be achieved after the death of God, let alone a "solution" to the crises that structure our present, it must include a turn toward these inhuman realities and a resituating and re-proportioning of the relative importance of human beings within them.

---

[23] For further reflections on climate change from this perspective, see Amitav Ghosh, *The Great Derangement* (Chicago: University of Chicago Press, 2016).

Chapter 5

VALUE

Obscure Human Fidelity

The reading of Jeffers developed thus far has left us with the following questions to consider in this final chapter: What sorts of values might emerge in adopting and practicing an inhumanist approach to life and death? Further, what sorts of changes does inhumanism entail at the level of the individual and at the level of the collective? I begin this chapter with an examination of two of Jeffers's early narratives, "Roan Stallion" and "The Tower Beyond Tragedy" in order to highlight the difficulties involved in adopting and sustaining an inhumanist perspective. I then turn to an examination of other writings by Jeffers that highlight the importance of ongoing practices of self-transformation and the role they play in transforming all-too-human subjectivities in a more inhumanist direction. Finally, I discuss how an inhumanist philosophy allows for a fresh reconsideration of the stakes of collective and political life.

* * *

Jeffers's early narrative poem "Roan Stallion" illustrates the risks and difficulties involved in contesting anthropocentric introversion.[1] The action of the poem centers around California, a young woman of mixed race, who is married to an abusive and heavy-drinking immigrant from Holland named Johnny. Living on an isolated ranch, California does her best to care for her daughter, Christine, while Johnny is often gone from the ranch and off

---

[1] There is a large secondary literature on this text. Two pieces of scholarship that I have found particularly insightful are: Tim Hunt, "Jeffers's 'Roan Stallion' and the Narrative of Nature," in *Robinson Jeffers: Dimensions of a Poet*, ed. Robert Brophy (New York: Fordham University Press, 1995), 64–83; and ShaunAnne Tangney, "'The mould to break away from': An Ecofeminist Reading of 'Roan Stallion,'" in *The Wild That Attracts Us: New Critical Essays on Robinson Jeffers*, ed. ShaunAnne Tangney (Albuquerque, NM: University of New Mexico Press, 2015), 141–60.

gambling. The titular animal of the piece refers to a horse that Johnny brings home one day as part of his winnings. The strong and beautiful horse represents for both California and Johnny something like a portal to a life outside their introverted existence on the ranch, but this "outside" is understood in different ways by the two characters. Johnny's goal is to use the stallion for breeding and to make money for personal economic gain and social standing, whereas California is drawn to the horse's overwhelming power, beauty, and independence, traits that allow her to glimpse a life beyond the restrictive limits of her relationship with Johnny.

Both characters exhibit quasi-zoophilic passions for the stallion, but again the form and end their respective affects take are starkly different.[2] When Johnny arranges to have the stallion breed with a mare, he and the horsemen watch the mating, with Johnny afterward crudely joking with the mare's owner that "to-morrow evening / I show her how the red fellow act, the big fellow" (CP 1, 188; SP, 124). Johnny and the men cruelly taunt the exhausted mare after the mating and deny her the time she needs to recover properly before forcing her to make the trek back home. California, who is also drawn to the act of mating and desires to see it in person, restrains herself from watching; and rather than displaying a crude and exploitative attitude toward the stallion's sexuality and power, California longs for him to be free of human control (she repeatedly imagines him being liberated and out "for a flag on the bare hills" [CP 1, 187; SP, 123]). As the narrative unfolds, it becomes clear that the stallion serves for California as a symbol or substitute for the divine and as the inspiration for a series of mystical experiences she has while out riding him beyond the confines of the ranch.

In the final scene of the poem, California reaches a breaking point in her dead-end and abusive relationship with Johnny. Upon returning from yet another bout of gambling, Johnny demands from California that she get drunk with him and have sex. California resists his demands and flees from the house toward the stallion's corral and climbs under the bars to join the horse. Following after her with his dog in tow, Johnny enters the stallion's corral and is subsequently attacked by the horse. Their daughter Christine hears the chaos and comes running to help, rifle in hand. She passes the rifle to California, assuming she will shoot the stallion and save Johnny. Instead,

---

2 In Jeffers's work, zoophilic themes and motifs are generally used to indicate a sort of more-than-human extroversion in his characters, a way of symbolically noting their opening to different passions beyond psychologically unhealthy interhuman erotic passions (the latter are often examined by Jeffers through symbolic analyses of incestuous relations and other forms of introversion).

California shoots the dog, which in turn allows the stallion to continue his attack on Johnny unobstructed. With Christine begging her to intervene, California waits until the stallion has killed Johnny and then, "moved by some obscure human fidelity" (CP 1, 198; SP, 134), finally shoots and kills the stallion. The event ends with California turning "on her little daughter the mask of a woman / Who has killed God" (CP 1, 198; SP, 134).

Both Johnny and California offer character studies in the struggle to break away from the dogmatic image of humanity. If the stallion represents something like the life and energies that circulate beyond the boundaries of humanity, neither California nor Johnny are, in the end, fully capable of turning themselves in that direction and transforming themselves accordingly. Johnny's abusive and exploitative disposition toward the horse links him to the more-than-human world in only the most negative and reductive ways, ultimately reorienting him to human affairs in view of profit and social power and thereby blocking him from exploring any transformative potentials that might arise at this intersection. California, by contrast, tries more sincerely to explore these sites of encounter and does seem to undergo something like a conversion in perspective and passions, but she is ultimately unable to sustain this conversion due in large part to the "obscure fidelity" that ties her to all-too-human perspectives and loyalties. Her killing of the stallion effectively functions to return her to the human fold and to prevent her from further exploring and living within the rift opened up by Johnny's death.

Breaking the Mold

In an essential narrative aside in "Roan Stallion," Jeffers underscores the importance of persisting with and carrying through on the gesture that California is unable to complete, noting that "Humanity is the mould to break away from [...] / The atom to be split" (CP 1, 189; SP, 125). And even though California herself fails to sustain this break (much like Barclay and several other protagonists in Jeffers's longer narrative poems[3]), there are occasional figures in his work who do accomplish such a break and who become something other than human, both in terms of their individual subjectivities and their loyalties. We see one important example of such success with the figure of Orestes in "The Tower Beyond Tragedy," Jeffers's reworking

---

3 As Jeffers explains, Barclay too "turned away from humanity and then turned back to it" (CL 2, 988). These words are from a letter to Elizabeth Bauer that Una transcribed for Jeffers. See James Karman's remarks on the background to the letter (CL 2, 989 n.1).

of Aeschylus's *Oresteia*.⁴ Here Jeffers reframes the interfamilial strife of this tragic cycle as a tale of excessive anthropocentric introversion and narcissism. In Jeffers's retelling of the story, he stalls the arc of the narrative just after Orestes has killed his mother, Clytemnestra, in revenge for her killing his father Agamemnon. And rather than having Athena subsequently intervene and institute justice as a means of putting an end to interfamilial and interhuman strife (as Aeschylus does), Jeffers turns the plot in a different direction, having Orestes's sister Electra try to seduce him. In Jeffers's retelling of the tragedy, Electra's desire is to have Orestes form a new royal union with her and take over the political power that previously belonged to their parents, thereby continuing the cycle of introversion and narcissism.

Orestes, however, refuses Electra's advances and refuses also to continue focusing exclusively on interhuman affairs. After traveling briefly to the forest and leaving the city behind, Orestes arrives at the conclusion that genuine peace resides not in the establishment of institutions of human justice, but in shifting his attention toward "the open world, the sea, and its wonders" (CP 1, 168). It is with this joint refusal and reorientation that Orestes accomplishes his turn outward and finally breaks the human mold. Like Diogenes of Sinope, Jeffers's Orestes locates his identity not within the confines of a single polis but within the cosmos as a whole, affirming his ontological and passional connections with the more-than-human world.⁵ In his "last labor" for humanity, Orestes recalls for Electra a vision he has had in which he discerns the reactive and incestuous passions animating humanity's actions:

> [...] all that we did or dreamed of [...] all loved or fought inward,
>   each one of the lost people
> Sought the eyes of another that another should praise him, sought
>   never his own but another's; the net of desire
> Had every nerve drawn to the center, so that they writhed like a full
>   draught of fishes . . .
> It is all turned inward, all your desires incestuous [...]. (CP 1, 176; SP, 112)⁶

---

4 The complete text of this work is found in CP 1, 119–78; it is partially excerpted in SP, 112–14.
5 Being described as "a homeless exile, to his country dead," Diogenes was asked where he came from and responded: "'I am a citizen of the world'" (Diogenes Laertius, *Lives of Eminent Philosophers*, 6.38, 6.61).
6 Jeffers explains the symbolic significance of incest in his work most clearly in letters to George Sterling (CL 1, 486–87) and George West (CL 1, 543–44).

The meaning of this vision remains unclear to Electra, confined as she is within the interhuman orbit from which Orestes has escaped. Refusing to explain the matter any further to her, Orestes instead voices the affirmative vision of planetary kinship and cosmic belonging he has gained. He tells Electra:

> [...] I have greater
> Kindred than dwell under a roof . . .
> [...] I remembered
> The knife in the stalk of my humanity; I drew and it broke; I entered
>   the life of the brown forest
> And the great life of the ancient peaks, the patience of stone, I felt the
>   changes in the veins
> In the throat of the mountain, a grain in many centuries, we have our
>   own time, not yours; and I was the stream
> Draining the mountain wood; and I the stag drinking; and I was the
>   stars,
> Boiling with light, wandering alone, each one the lord of his own sum-
>   mit; and I was the darkness
> Outside the stars, I included them, they were a part of me. I was man-
>   kind also, a moving lichen
> On the cheek of the round stone [...] they have not made words for it,
>   to go behind things, beyond hours and ages [...]
> [...] how can I express the excellence I have found [...]. (CP 1,
>   176–77; SP, 113)[7]

The question of how, precisely, Orestes makes this shift remains something of a critical limit for Jeffers in this early text. Orestes's conversion is neither thematized nor even roughly sketched. It is as if Orestes has achieved

---

7 Jeffers's glosses Orestes's gesture with the following words: "Orestes [...] identifies himself with the whole divine nature of things; earth, man and stars, the mountain forest and the running streams; they are all one existence, one organism. He perceives this, and that himself is included in it, identical with it. This perception is his tower beyond the reach of tragedy; because, whatever may happen, the great organism will remain forever immortal and immortally beautiful" ("'Tower Beyond Tragedy': Poet and Playwright Tells How He Wrote Drama Based on Greek Stories," in CL 3, 943). Orestes's claims about kinship here are echoed by Jeffers himself in a late unpublished poem in which he claims his own "natural choices": "I am truly much nearer kin to the trees and the sea-mountain / And this wild shore, than to man or woman" (CP 4, 550).

in a single gesture[8] an insight that has allowed him to leap from a humanist perspective and way of life to a radical inhumanism; or perhaps there were intervening steps and Orestes (or Jeffers himself at this point in his poetic career) is unable or unwilling to elaborate them as part of his last labor to his fellow human beings. Either way, we have to look beyond this early sketch of an effort to break the mold of humanity if we wish to consider whether there is any need to prepare oneself for such an effort or undertake training in order to sustain it.

Hints that such preparation and training might be needed can be gained by returning to "The Humanist's Tragedy," Jeffers's brief retelling of Euripides's *Bacchae*, which I discussed in Chapter 4. There we saw that, as Pentheus spies on the women engaged in Bacchic revelry on Mount Cithaeron, Dionysus himself walks among the women and offers them guidance on how to enter into the "opening" and "wild strait gate-way" (CP 1, 381) they have found during their festive rites. As Dionysus explains, this opening is a portal to the "peace" and "sacred beauty" of things (CP 1, 382). He tells the revelers that peace awaits all individuals at death, but that it is also possible to gain access to the beauty of things while we are alive. If we do so while alive, Dionysus explains, we can have a conscious share in this beauty and even learn to engage it (and this is, to be sure, the *summum bonum* that motivates Jeffers's entire work). Dionysus goes on to tell the women that there are many ways to break free of oneself and enter the beauty of things. He suggests that "Wine and lawlessness, art and music, love, self-torture, religion, / Are means," but notes that they are not necessary, and that "contemplation [alone] will do it" (CP 1, 381).[9] What is needed above all else is a sustained effort "to break human collectedness," and this is something "the least shepherd on Cythaeron, if he dares, might do" (CP 1, 381). In preferring contemplation to the other practices he mentions, Dionysus casts a critical eye on those who take his rites as indicating that spontaneous and occasional acts of excess will in themselves serve to break human collectedness or sustain a relation and creative engagement with the beauty of things. He tells the women: "you being neophyte all […] / Are indeed somewhat wild, somewhat too drunken" (CP 1, 381).

---

8 Orestes himself notes that his conversion is sudden: "Because I have suddenly awakened, I will not waste inward / Upon humanity, having found a fairer object" (CP 1, 175).

9 See Jeffers's related remarks on contemplation as a form of the good life in "Cruel Falcon" (CP 2, 412; SP, 501).

Dionysus's remarks to the neophytes can help us to see more clearly the stakes of the various experiments in limit behaviors (extreme sexual behaviors, violent and aggressive actions, attempt at radical withdrawal and social alienation, etc.) that Jeffers explores with the protagonists of his longer narratives. The chief characters that populate these works (especially in the early portions of his career) are often used by Jeffers to experiment with various strategies for breaking human collectedness and crossing the threshold into the beauty of things. As I noted above, nearly all of the protagonists of these poems fail to accomplish their desired breakthrough. Perhaps the chief reason why many of these characters fail to sustain this break and are unable to create and enact a form of life on the other side of the human is that they have not *practiced* their way into it in a sustained manner. The (mistaken) assumption most of the characters seem to make is that some kind of limit experience or radical transgression will itself suffice for a change of perspective and a subjective transformation. Moreover, these characters give inadequate attention to the corresponding practices that might allow them to continue along the path of transformation and sustain a different mode of subjectivity over the long term. The failed experiments in Jeffers's longer poems might thus be taken to suggest that, without sustained practice aimed at breaking the human mold, an "obscure human fidelity" will recapture us and lead us back into the all-too-human fold.

In "Sign-Post" (CP 2, 418; SP, 504) Jeffers considers at more length the sorts of practices that might lead to achieving and sustaining a genuine break from human collectedness, practices that would thereby provide the space needed to become a different kind of subject. The poem is initially framed in such a way as to make us think that spiritual conversion is a matter of finding our way back home to our true selves and to our essential human nature, with its opening lines stating: "Civilized, crying how to be human again: this will tell you how." But Jeffers instead directs us (and perhaps himself, too) away from ourselves and from humanity and toward inhuman affairs: "Turn outward, love things, not men, turn right away from humanity, / Let that doll lie." In making the turn outward, the poet endeavors to move the reader's eyes and attention away from the human and instead toward the beauty of the lilies (recalling Matthew 6:28 and Luke 12:27), to the divine majesty of the silent rock, and all the way to the distant stars, allowing the reader gradually to "climb the great ladder out of the pit" of oneself and humanity.

In traversing this inhuman path away from humanity and outward to more-than-human life, inorganic matter, and the vast depths of cosmic space, the poet suggests to the reader that the heart will follow the eyes and that one will learn to love what one sees there, for "things are so beautiful." Having one's heart thus attuned and being washed in this transhuman beauty also has the gradual effect of transforming the self toward an inhuman form: "For what we love, we grow to it, we share its nature." Thus, if we adopt the poet's recommended path, in striving to become human again, we must gradually morph into *in*human subjects and learn to refocus our attention and loyalties on *in*human majesties.

After we have undertaken such practices of attention for some time, the poet would have us eventually return our gaze to humanity and recognize that human affairs also have a place in this broader inhuman order and that they also possess their own beauty and deserve our love. In effect, Jeffers is here proposing nothing less than a new, demythologized way of understanding and practicing the *entolē megalē*, the greatest commandment: loving the one God (that is, the inhuman beauty of things as a whole) first and foremost, and also our human neighbors as ourselves.[10] It is only after we have walked this path "at length," the poet suggests, that we are "free" to be reborn and become genuinely different selves. But this rebirth is not to be understood as being biological in origin but instead as deriving from "the rock and the air," from being attuned to and learning to love the inhuman elements. Becoming "human again" is thus, paradoxically, a matter of letting go of the human, turning one's heart outward, and learning to become more and more *in*human.

Earnest Lives

We might wonder, though, what sorts of values correspond to this shift toward inhuman subjectivity? Is there such a thing as an inhumanist mode of being in the world, or a corresponding way of life? Jeffers addresses these issues forthrightly in a poem entitled "The Answer" (CP 2, 536; SP, 522). Here, he situates the question of individual values against the backdrop of ongoing interhuman violence and widespread cultural decline. How to live well in such circumstances? For Jeffers, this is a particularly pressing question not just because it reflects his contemporary circumstances but because he believes that the general cultural decline he is witnessing cannot be simply stopped or reversed and that many of his future readers will be confronted with a similar set of phenomena and concerns. Jeffers maintains throughout his mature poetry that, just as living organisms go through a cycle of birth, growth, life, decline, death, and decay, so do cultures and civilizations.[11] All

---

10 See Matthew 22:36–40 and CP 4, 412.
11 Jeffers suggests that this idea is a "common and obvious one" for our epoch, but he also attributes it in part to his reading of Flinders Petrie and Oswald Spengler

things, whether individual or collective, are for Jeffers strapped inextricably to the Wheel of Fortune (see Chapter 1). The ethical task, then, is to live well, not just in times of healthy growth and ascension but also in the more challenging times of protracted decline and violence. In such times, he counsels: "When open violence appears, to avoid it with honor or choose the least ugly faction […] [to] be merciful and uncorrupted and not wish for evil." Above all else, it is essential under such circumstances to "keep one's own integrity" (CP 2, 536; SP, 522).

The concern with maintaining one's integrity is a commonly tread theme in Jeffers's work, and it speaks to his fundamental awareness of the need to live in such a way that we guard our hearts from the forces that would sweep us up into the senseless violence and aimless drifting that characterize modern civilization. In one of Jeffers's popular early poems, "Shine, Perishing Republic" (CP 1, 15; SP, 23), he reflects on the challenge of maintaining one's integrity in the face of war. Writing ostensibly to his children (and, of course, his reading public as well, for the poem was not ultimately kept private for his children), he notes that as "America settles in the mould of its vulgarity, heavily thickening to empire," it is essential for them to "keep their distance from the thickening center" and to avoid having their integrity corrupted by the empire. He reminds his children that "corruption / Never has been compulsory, when the cities lie at the monster's feet there are left the mountains." Elsewhere, Jeffers challenges readers to hold fiercely to the ideal of freedom against the luxuries that threaten to further erode independence in the name of mass conformity and consumerism. Maintaining such intellectual independence and physical distance from the violence and emptiness of the dominant culture is, for Jeffers, an essential prerequisite for the kind of "force and self-discipline," the "many refusals" and "few assertions" that allow us to "assure ourselves / Freedom and integrity in life" (CP 2, 531; SP, 521).

For Jeffers, the genuine counterforce to a corrupt and trivial life is not so much one that is taken up with grand projects but rather is a form of life that is lived *earnestly*. The exemplars for such a life in his poems are most often animals, beings whose lives flow with the recurrent patterns and rhythms of daily and seasonal life. Animals go about their business of living with a kind of focus and quiet nobility that is often lacking in our lives, distracted as we tend to be by trivia that have little or nothing to do with life's necessities. In

---

(CP 4, 396). Jeffers's most succinct poetic reflections on this theme are found in "Prescription of Painful Ends" (CP 3, 14; SP 561). Note also that Jeffers's conjectures about the decline and fall of Western civilization are coupled with "the hope for a better one" (CP 4, 406).

"Boats in a Fog" (CP 1, 110; SP, 105) Jeffers compares the childish charms provided by popular entertainment ("Sports and gallantries, the stage, the arts, the antics of dancers / The exuberant voices of music") with the beauty and nobility of the soberer life of "bitter earnestness / That makes beauty." This latter, more "essential reality / Of creatures going about their business among the equally / Earnest elements of nature" can be seen he suggests in the everyday occurrence of the "flight of pelicans" (a familiar but no less remarkable phenomenon for someone who lives on the ocean, as Jeffers does, and sees the daily comings and goings of these birds). But it can also be found among those human beings who earnestly immerse themselves in the act of living and the more permanent rhythms of existence. The "boats in a fog" of this poem refers to fishing boats that Jeffers witnesses solemnly and cautiously going about their work despite being engulfed by a thick fog bank that has made their travel perilous. He finds another example of a human life lived earnestly when he witnesses an elderly Chinese man "gathering seaweed from the sea-rocks" for food and spreading it flat to dry on the edge of a meadow, a perennial task carried out between "the solemn presences of land and ocean" (CP 1, 90; SP, 98). This is what Jeffers refers to as a life of "pure action," a good life that is "sharp- / Set between the throat and the knife" (CP 2, 412; SP, 501). For Jeffers, a life of earnest work and intentional action is far preferable to one of "pleasant peace and security" wherein "the soul in a man begins to die" (CP 2, 412; SP, 501).

Jeffers's interest in earnest living also helps to clarify what might otherwise appear at first glance to be a kind of uncritical and nostalgic pastoralism in certain portions of his work. Take, for example, Jeffers's remarks on the way of life he encountered on the Monterey coast upon first arriving there in 1914. He notes that it was there for the first time in his life he saw people living "amid magnificent unspoiled scenery—essentially as they did in the Idyls or the Sagas, or in Homer's Ithaca. Here was life purged of its ephemeral accretions" (CP 4, 392; SP, 715). Of course, the Monterey coast in the early 1900s was by no means an untrammeled wilderness that had historically been devoid of people; there were plenty of people who inhabited the area, and Jeffers knew well that Indigenous peoples had lived in the region long before the arrival of settlers and had had their way of life violently interrupted by colonialism and the establishment of the nearby Carmel Mission. The key to Jeffers's appreciation of this section of coastline is based less on its supposedly pristine form and more on the fact that he saw people living *earnest* lives there (as opposed to the empty and aimless way of life he witnessed and fell into himself in the city of Los Angeles where he was previously living).

> Men were riding after cattle, or plowing the headland, hovered by white sea-gulls, as they have done for thousands of years, and will for thousands of years to come. Here was contemporary life that was also permanent life; and not shut from the modern world but conscious of it and related to it; capable of expressing its spirit, but unencumbered by the mass of poetically irrelevant details and complexities that make a civilization. (CP 4, 392; SP, 715)

Jeffers's description of such lives as having the characteristic of being "permanent" is the key to understanding his remarks here. He is not celebrating a pastoral way of life as such (after all, he did not live this way himself and it is hardly a permanent feature of human existence), but rather is marking the difference between contemporary "civilized" life based on trivial interests and a truer and more earnest life that continues "onward the same / Though Dynasties pass" (to recall Thomas Hardy's apt phrasing).[12]

Such (relative) permanence is, as I have noted, one of the central characteristics that Jeffers sought to achieve with his own poetry. And it is here that we can see how the writing of poetry serves as one of the contemplative practices whereby one becomes more like the inhuman realities one loves. For Jeffers, poetry should have little to say about "fashionable and momentary" (CP 1, 90; SP, 98) things and treat the ephemeral as having only "news-value" (CP 4, 391; SP, 714). Poetry's proper material is derived from "permanent things […] things temporally / Of great dimension, things continually renewed or always present" (CP 1, 90; SP, 98). Thus, poetry is attuned to human and more-than-human matters inasmuch as they belong to these more permanent cycles and modes of existence. This is why a life lived simply and earnestly by animals, nature, and human beings are equipollent in their beauty and poetic worth; and it is also why Jeffers's poetry carries the same simple, earnest quality: his poetry is but one more effort to live and create in a way that "equals the mountains" in the (relative) permanence of their "past and future" (CP 1, 90; SP, 98). If earnest living on the part of human beings not only reflects the inhuman world in all of its beauty but on occasion equals and even adds to that beauty in some fundamental way, so much the better. Such a life would be both a good life and a remarkable one. There can be little doubt that Jeffers endeavored to create poetry of this remarkable sort, but he did not concern himself overmuch with whether his own contribution or that of his fellow human beings rises to the level of being remarkable. The majesty of

---

12 For more of Jeffers's poetic reflections on this theme, see especially "The Wind-Struck Music" (CP 2, 520–21; SP, 516–17).

inhuman reality is sufficient unto itself. And if we but attend to it and strive to live in accord with its permanence, we will over time build a life that is well-lived and gather all the subjective resources we need to face life's difficulties.[13]

Dying Well

An inhumanist stance focuses not just on learning to live well but also learning to die well. Beyond simply assuaging common fears about death, Jeffers seeks to reframe the human experience of death in view of what he sees as its salvific and consolatory dimensions. This approach to death is exemplified most notably at end of the short narrative piece "Margrave," where Jeffers describes in detail the demise of young Walter Margrave, who is sentenced to death for the murder of a young girl.[14] With four days to wait until his execution, the dread and horror of death looms large in Walter's mind. When he is eventually hanged, though, death arrives as a kind of salvation. The noose snaps his neck, severing the connection between mind and body, their previously conjoined consciousnesses going their respective ways. The severed mind briefly flashes with a "paradisal light / Like the wild birth of a star, but crying in bewilderment and suddenly extinguished," whereas the disconnected body experiences something like the feeling of "satisfied love, a wave of hard warmth and joy" that eventually runs cold and turns to darkness. Jeffers then describes the slow fading of the mind's consciousness, its dreams, and eventual disintegration and dissolution.

> After a time of darkness
> The dreams that follow upon death came and subsided, like fibrillar twitchings
> Of the nerves unorganizing themselves; and some of the small dreams were delightful and some, slight miseries,
> But nothing intense; then consciousness wandered home from the cell to the molecule, was utterly dissolved and changed;
> Peace was the end of the play, so far as concerns humanity. Oh beautiful capricious little savior,
> Death, the gay child with the gipsy eyes, to avoid you for a time I think is virtuous, to fear you is insane. (CP 2, 171; SP, 393)

---

13 On these points, see also Jeffers's October 1, 1934 letter to Sister Mary James Power (CL 2, 364–65).
14 See Chapter 3 for further discussion of this poem.

With the dissolution of consciousness and the concomitant dissolution of the bodily organism, human beings are once again returned to the play of the earth and the cosmos, "rolled round in earth's diurnal course / With rocks, and stones, and trees" (to recall Wordsworth). This return in death to the elements, while acknowledged by all thinkers and poets more or less begrudgingly, is for Jeffers something to be joyfully affirmed, for it constitutes both our salvation and consolation. It is our salvation in the sense that it heals any painful rift between our consciousness and the beauty of things that might have plagued us. It is our consolation in the sense that our bodies will be transformed upon death into other beings and relations and will continue in another form in the great planetary and cosmic drama that precedes and exceeds us.[15]

That returning to the elements could be a form of salvation and consolation is given further expression in a lyric entitled "Vulture" (CP 3, 462). In this piece, which was written shortly before his death and left unpublished, Jeffers recounts an experience of stopping to rest for an extended period during a walk and noticing a vulture circling and inspecting him from above. Jeffers decides to lie still and allow the vulture to descend closer until he can hear its flight and catch sight of the bird's face. Eventually, he signals to the bird that he is not dead and breaks their connection. While the possibility of becoming prey for another animal is often thought to be the worst imaginable end for a human being, Jeffers instead sees great beauty in such a fate and in the bird itself: its feathers, its majestic flight, its embeddedness in the larger beauty of things. Jeffers tells us that he was "sorry to have disappointed" the bird: "To be eaten by that beak and become part of him, to share those wings and those eyes—/ What a sublime end of one's body, what an enskyment; what a life after death."

Jeffers's affirmation of "enskyment" and his own edibility amounts to a sharp refusal of what Val Plumwood describes as the "story of human hyperseparation from nature" that characterizes dominant Western cultural narratives about death.[16] In affirming the possibility of one's potentially becoming flesh for another being, and in affirming our belonging to the basic earthly cycle of consuming and being consumed, we give up the project of "guarding ourselves jealously and keeping ourselves apart" from the earth and instead

---

15 In writing the inscription for his gravestone, Jeffers wishes to remind his readers: "I am not dead, I have only become inhuman […] I admired the beauty / While I was human, now I am part of the beauty" (CP 2, 125; SP, 372).

16 Val Plumwood, *The Eye of the Crocodile*, ed. Lorraine Shannon (Canberra: ANU E Press, 2012), 18.

give ourselves back to the beings, processes, and relations that have constituted and nurtured us throughout our lives.[17] As Jeffers writes: "death comes and plucks us: We become part of the living earth / And wind and water whom we so loved. We are they" (CP 3, 412; SP, 685). When Jeffers finally passed away on January 20, 1962, he was cremated and his ashes were scattered in the sea that formed and nurtured his life and thought. He expressed his wish not to be buried in a coffin and "rot in the earth" but instead to end by roaring "up in flame," which he had done so often "with love or fury" throughout his life (CP 3, 480).

Inhumanism and the Political

Jeffers's poetry contains substantive reflections on the art of existence that correspond to what we might call the *individual* or *subjective* level. The foregoing considerations on this theme in the present chapter have only scratched the surface of this dimension of Jeffers's work but should, I hope, provide a helpful way of grasping its stakes and main outlines. But what about the art of *political*, or *collective* existence? What does Jeffers's poetry have to offer concerning this register of life *in common*? It might seem rather crude to ask such a question of a poet, to demand that a poet offer us a "politics" or some vision for life in common—after all, it is not at all clear that the task of the poet is to be a "political" thinker in any traditional sense of the word. Yet, inquiring about the political dimensions of Jeffers's poetic work is not an unfair or unfitting gesture for he himself injects consideration of political matters explicitly into his work. So, the concern here is not about the propriety of inquiring into the political dimensions of Jeffers's thought but rather of seeking the best point of entry for understanding what is at issue in his work in this register.

One mistake to avoid in this vein is to view Jeffers's work as "an attempt to have poetry function in support of political action or to advance a particular political position or vision"—which is to say, following Tim Hunt's apt suggestion, we should not read him as an ideologue for a standard political position or framework.[18] Rather, as I suggested in Chapter 2, Jeffers's work is better understood as an attempt to redirect our attention and loyalties beyond the coordinates offered by the established political order. For not only are the ruling ideologies complicit in the worst forms of violence (a point Jeffers often

---

17 Plumwood, *Eye of the Crocodile*, 19.
18 Tim Hunt, "The Politics that Aren't in the Poetry of Robinson Jeffers," https://tahunt.com/robinson-jeffers-modern-poetry/the-politics-that-arent-in-the-poetry-of-robinson-jeffers/.

raised), they also orient us away from the matters of permanence and beauty to which Jeffers's poetry seeks to direct us.

I would suggest that the most lasting and significant political contribution Jeffers's work makes to political matters is that he allows us to catch sight from a fresh angle of what is at stake in our collective lives. In view of the political struggles and coordinates with which most of his readers today will likely be aligned (I assume that the bulk of Jeffers's readers and readers of the present book will find themselves somewhere along the spectrum of progressive and leftist politics, especially inasmuch as that political inclination links up with discourses and movements related to the ethics and politics of the more-than-human world), Jeffers's work is extraordinarily helpful for rethinking the teleological and optimistic tendencies that tend to characterize this orientation. Movements for social justice and progress generally have their philosophical origins in perfectionistic views of natural and human cultural evolution, views which lean toward the adoption of political tactics and strategies aimed at long-term progress and incremental change. One of the more sobering challenges of the present age is coming to grips with the idea that political optimism and progressive reformism of this sort, while admirable in spirit, are no longer tenable. Not only has interhuman politics proven time and again over the past several centuries to contain no progressive arc toward justice, but the longer-term ecological future of the planet threatens to undermine the temporal conditions required for long-term progress to unfold. Simply put, there appears to be no march toward justice in human history; and even if we were to discern the traces of such a thread, human civilization and political institutions in their current and familiar form are running out of time to accomplish any such progressive goals. Political realism today demands that we adopt a fundamentally non-teleological and non-progressive perspective, one that seeks to enact political changes where possible but without the sense that such changes carry any historical necessity or belong to some larger, progressive arc guiding the unfolding of history.

Jeffers is an important ally in trying to accomplish this shift in perspective, as he had long jettisoned any such political optimism from his work, living as he did through the mass violence of two World Wars and witnessing early forms of ecological decline. As I noted earlier in this chapter, Jeffers held a non-teleological and cyclical view of both natural and social history in which both organisms and societies as a whole are subject to birth, life, decline, and death. On this account, nothing can escape the Wheel of Fortune, not even large-scale civilizations like our own. Thus, any politics grounded on faith in the teleological progression of human civilization toward increased justice and liberation misconstrues the fundamental nature of things. Again, this kind of cyclical perspective does not entail that progress never occurs, or that fighting for justice is inherently naïve. Rather, it means that in turning our efforts and attention toward interhuman politics to address injustices and reconfigure social relations, it is necessary to adjust our guiding assumptions about what might be accomplished in this register over the long term. Movements for social change, no matter how much in the moral right they might be, cannot be assured of success in the long run; and there are no guarantees that social, cultural, and economic conditions will always be ripe for bringing social change to fruition. There might even be times when a given culture is rushing headlong into decline and cannot be diverted from that path except temporarily (which is, effectively, Jeffers's judgment regarding the present moment of American civilization in particular and Western civilization more generally). But even in these sorts of dark times, there is no reason we cannot live with integrity, resist injustice wherever it is possible to do so, and build beautiful and worthwhile lives in common in the midst of decline.

Jeffers suggests that the source of much of the unnecessary trouble and strife in our collective, cultural lives stems from giving excessive value and attention to interhuman affairs. As a counterstrategy, he counsels turning to the splendor of the inhuman world: "I wish you could find the secure value, / The all-heal I found when a former time hurt me to the heart, / The splendor of inhuman things: you would not be looking at each others' throats with your knives" (CP 2, 516). Now, if turning outward in this manner were simply a matter of ignoring social injustices or blithely allowing political violence to go unchecked, there would be little to recommend Jeffers's perspective. But what makes this outward shift worth considering is that an inhumanist reorientation of our attention and loyalties is presented by Jeffers as a way of transforming not just our individual selves but our social relations as well. Jeffers maintains, and I think rightly so, that if we learn to anchor ourselves in the inhuman majesty of things, and to find "the secure value" there, we will be able increasingly to turn away from the petty antagonisms and strife that tend to pervade many of our interhuman interactions. Learning to love the beauty of inhuman things is, thus, not a matter of ignoring or denigrating our fellow human beings but is a way of finding the perspective necessary to see them and ourselves anew, as but one part of that larger inhuman beauty, and striving in a corresponding way to articulate collective ideals and ways of life that allow us to become worthy of our belonging to its majesty and grandeur.

It must be acknowledged, though, that Jeffers's political vision, inasmuch as it eschews dominant political ideologies, involves risks and invites misunderstanding. As I noted in Chapter 2, Jeffers's near-total rejection of the dominant ideologies and movements of his era (reactionary, conservative, moderate, progressive, and radical alike) led to him being labeled a political pariah by many of his contemporaries. With the distance of some six decades since his death now behind us, though, we might be better poised today to set such critical judgments aside and appreciate the deeper political dimensions of his stance. First, it should be clear that Jeffers rejects the socialist and communist politics of his era not because he is in favor of capitalism and socioeconomic inequality but because he thinks that progressive and radical movements fail to ground themselves in the sort of inhumanist values and loyalties he believes are requisite for living well. Conversely, Jeffers rejects the reactionary movements and conservatism of his era, not because he is committed to an optimistic vision of progress, but because this politics seeks to retrieve a past that is in many respects one well gone. The past to which the conservatives of his era wished to return was littered with the horrors of slavery, colonialism, and the bloody acts of culture that Jeffers often recalls for us. And he rejects more moderate forms of centrism and liberalism for their naïve faith in reformism and their inability to direct us away from the trivial lives promoted by the dominant culture and the narrow focus of modern life. In brief, the dominant values on offer across the political spectrum reflect, for Jeffers, a people who have failed to find the "secure value," who have sought truth, goodness, and beauty within the narrow confines of interhuman affairs rather than in the larger majesty and beauty of things; and it is on these grounds that he rejects them *in toto*.

In brief, by Jeffers's account, modern society has encouraged us to fundamentally misorient ourselves. Our "souls" have become invested in and predominately attuned to the ephemera on offer in the interhuman sphere; and the consumerist lifestyle that corresponds to this soul orientation reinforces the structures of exploited labor, oppression, and cruelty that make city life possible. Jeffers maintains that if we were to orient our souls otherwise, toward the beauty of things, the earth would be "poorer by many beautiful agonies" (CP 2, 418). In turning away from the emptiness and violence of city life, Jeffers is not of course encouraging us to seek a politics of easy equality, comfortable living, or social isolation. Rather he is counseling a way of life that uncenters the human mind from itself (CP 3, 399; SP 676) and opens itself to the majesty and potentialities of the inhuman. In one of his rare public lectures ("The Poet in a Democracy," CP 4, 399–406), Jeffers elaborates on this sense of politics by way of the classical ideal of freedom. His invocation of this ideal, though, is far from a paean to free markets or to individual egoism. Valuing freedom from an inhumanist perspective means instead valuing our ability to resist the "purse-seine" net that seeks to drag all of us into conformity with dominant political ideals, whether they are reactionary, liberal, or radical. It means valuing the freedom to open ourselves to more-than-human potentials, to the wide array of inhuman realities that lie outside the dominant coordinates, and to build a way of life that emerges in and through an engagement with those realities and their beauty and permanence. It means valuing a politics grounded in genuine love and friendship for our fellow human beings, a politics that delivers all of us into a space where such experiments in living well are held open. To love one's neighbor as one loves oneself is, from Jeffers's perspective, to safeguard that same difficult and dangerous freedom for others that one should, ideally, seek to preserve for oneself.

CONCLUSION: INHUMANISM

In October of 1947, at the age of 60, Jeffers submitted to Random House the manuscript for his penultimate and perhaps most notorious book of poetry, *The Double Axe and Other Poems*. Written in the midst and aftermath of World War II, the manuscript contained scathing criticisms of US foreign policy and its involvement in the war; it also included harshly negative remarks about President Roosevelt's political judgment and physical paralysis. Saxe Commins, his longtime editor at Random House, was so taken aback by the manuscript's content that he requested from Jeffers substantial edits to several poems and removal of several others.[1] Even after Jeffers had complied with most of these requests, Random House decided to append a Publisher's Note to the beginning of *The Double Axe* voicing their "disagreement over some of the political views pronounced by the poet in this volume" when it finally appeared in print in July of 1948.[2]

Considerable scholarly attention has been focused on this dispute, with many of Jeffers's supporters viewing Random House's editorial interventions as a scandalous instance of suppressing free speech and artistic creativity. Jeffers himself, though, seems to have taken the matter largely in stride, complying with most of Commins's requests and offering mild pushback on others.[3] Along with the retractions and revisions he made to the main body of the work, Jeffers also substantially revised his original Preface, making it considerably shorter and removing several important philosophical reflections. Fortunately, the original, unpublished Preface has been preserved and is readily accessible (CP 4, 418–21; SP 719–22). It includes a pellucid

---

1 See Dorothy Commins, *What Is an Editor? Saxe Commins at Work* (Chicago: University of Chicago Press, 1978), 121–31, for the entire correspondence from Commins.
2 "Publishers Note," in *The Double Axe & Other Poems* (New York: Random House, 1948), viii.
3 For Jeffers's correspondence with Commins on matters related to *The Double Axe*, see CL 506–7, 520–22, and 524–34. Tim Hunt has carefully collated the various drafts and revisions to both Prefaces in CP 5, 981–987 and 997–1001.

exposition of Jeffers's mature philosophy of inhumanism and also offers some of his clearest insights into how this way of thinking can address the challenges of finding meaning and beauty amid life's difficulties. In this concluding chapter, I want to examine both Prefaces in order to review some of the key themes of the previous chapters and to return to the issue of evil with which I began my reading of Jeffers.

In the shorter, published Preface to *The Double Axe,* Jeffers remarks that the book presents "a certain philosophical attitude" that he calls "Inhumanism" (CP 4, 428). This attitude, he tells us, is based on a shift in emphasis from "man to not-man," a turning outward from the human world to the "transhuman" or more-than-human world. In the original version of the Preface, Jeffers explains that the inhumanist turn is founded on a twofold gesture: the recognition and affirmation of "the astonishing beauty of things and their living wholeness," and a "rational acceptance" and awareness of the notion that humanity is "neither central nor important" in the cosmic scope of things (CP 4, 418; SP, 719). This inhumanist framework, Jeffers notes, came to him at the end of war in 1914 and has been tested repeatedly in his work against the realities of war and peace in the subsequent decades. Jeffers is thus marking here the absolute centrality of inhumanism to his entire mature poetic project, the overarching philosophical question and concern that structures it from beginning to end. And it is because this perspective has passed the test of time for Jeffers that he can say with some assurance that he believes inhumanism "has truth and value" (CP 4, 418; SP 719)—that it can be objectively defended and argued for, and that it can serve as the normative foundation for a distinct and worthwhile way of life (themes I discussed at some length in Chapters 4 and 5).

Jeffers notes further in the original Preface that his inhumanist philosophy is not meant to introduce ideas that are utterly novel to modern human beings. To some extent, we already know and feel these truths about our own insignificance and about the grandeur of the transhuman world; but we nevertheless resist placing them in the foreground of our thoughts and actions. Further, they have failed to be realized, Jeffers suggests, in "any previous one of the ten thousand religions and philosophies" (CP 4, 418; SP, 719) that populate human history. But what is the source of this failure to bring our individual and collective lives into harmony with inhumanist truth and values?

Jeffers points toward two distinct but related obstacles on the path to an inhumanist way of life and thought. The first concerns our *collective immaturity*. Here Jeffers suggests that much as an infant takes itself to be of "central and primary importance" (CP 4, 418; SP, 719) in family life, so too do civilized, adult human beings tacitly assume themselves to be of central and primary importance in a planetary and cosmic context. After Copernicus,

Darwin, and the various scientific and intellectual revolutions we have passed through, such a perspective is of course entirely untenable; yet the self-image that functions in the background of our daily lives has yet to catch up to these facts and assume an "adult habit of thought" (CP 4, 418; SP, 719).[4] Thus, what inhumanism calls for is something like a second Enlightenment—*encore un effort!*—this time to raise ourselves out of our self-imposed immaturity in regard to affirming the relative (in)significance of human existence and our decentered status. In contrast to the previous European Enlightenment, the goal here is not just to wrest intellectual and practical autonomy away from those who would usurp it (although Jeffers's work certainly presupposes the importance of something like this gesture, as I noted at the end of Chapter 5), but rather to use that hard-won freedom of thought and life to recognize our immersion in inhuman realities that enable and condition our existence from the ground up.

The second obstacle is our *collective introversion*. Similar to a psychologically unhealthy individual who suffers from extreme inner strife and excessive self-focus, Jeffers argues that modern civilized human beings suffer from being excessively turned inward on themselves and their collective interactions, interests, and affairs. The vast majority of our energies in the context of civilized living are, he notes, "devoted to self-interference, self-frustration, self-incitement, self-tickling, self-worship" (CP 4, 419; SP, 720). We have arrived at this extreme form of introversion, Jeffers maintains, because the daily tasks of living have been made so extraordinarily easy for so many of us, leaving us with excess energies we "discharge onto each other" (CP 4, 419; SP, 720) in largely unhealthy ways.[5] In challenging our collective introversion, Jeffers is not proposing, of course, to exit altogether from human relationships—they are "necessary and desirable," he notes, but he is arguing that we need not focus on them to the excessive and exclusive degree that civilized life encourages. This is precisely the sort of introversion Jeffers critically targets in so

---

4 It is important to note that the particular form of collective immaturity targeted here ought not be universally attributed to human beings; Jeffers's critical remarks are clearly aimed at the dominant intellectual traditions of the West in particular. Conversely, the achievement of the sort of inhumanist maturity Jeffers has in mind can undoubtedly be found to various degrees in minor cultures beyond the West. Thus, we might see the inhumanist project as one in which Westerners must finally learn to join those who have been walking this path for some time now.

5 Jeffers is, of course, well aware that this ease is built on the backs of countless domestic and international laborers as well as the exploitation of the more-than-human world. What he is trying to diagnose here is the intensification of an illness that plagues individuals who are comfortably ensconced inside an affluent modern culture.

many of his poems—the mold that so many of his characters struggle to break out of. Jeffers takes pains to emphasize that this call to turn away from collective immaturity and introversion is not a matter of misanthropy or life pessimism; rather, it is intended to outline what he calls a "rule of conduct" based on a "reasonable detachment" from the narrow orbit of interhuman concerns (CP 4, 428). It is the failure to adopt and enact such a rule of conduct, I argued in Chapter 5, that renders many of Jeffers's protagonists incapable of sustaining a break with the dogmatic image of humanity inherited from the dominant culture. Such "detachment" and reorientation toward the more-than-human world, if it is to be sustained for any length of time, is not merely the result of an instantaneous shift in intellectual perspective but follows from a series of repeated practices and the gradual, intentional formation of an inhumanist subjective disposition.

There are any number of life practices through which one might enact this rule of conduct and become more attuned to the inhuman beauty that surrounds us. Jeffers proposes that the excess energies we direct on each other might be redirected to this goal, perhaps by taking up such practices as contemplation, art, science, and other forms of earnest and sincere living that turn us outward.[6] Of course, we need not be naïve about what might be accomplished in making this sort of turn in our subjective and collective lives. Jeffers is under no illusion that we will entirely overcome our immaturity and introversion, for these all-too-human characteristics are not mere by-products of civilized life; instead, they are deep-rooted tendencies among human beings that precede, but are intensified by, civilization. Adopting an inhumanist perspective and way of life can only change the relative proportions of our attention and the fidelities and passions that organize our daily lives. But by minimizing our introversion and self-aggrandizement and maximizing our efforts to find meaning and value beyond civilized life in the more-than-human world, we will gradually become different kinds of people and become correspondingly capable of living different, and more beautiful, lives.

As I have just noted, the turn outward toward the more-than-human world is not intended to have us withdraw entirely from human fellowship. Indeed, the sustained practice of turning outward allows us to subsequently return our gaze to ourselves and our fellow human beings through inhumanist lenses and values. Thus disposed, we can learn better to balance our interest

---

6 As Jeffers notes in his address, "Themes in My Poems," the happiest and freest man is "the scientist investigating nature, or the artist admiring it; the person who is interested in things that are not human. Or if he is interested in human things, let him regard them objectively, as a very small part of the great music" (CP 4, 412).

in interhuman relations with a passion for the more-than-human world (of which human affairs are but one small part). In the previous chapter, I suggested that Jeffers can be read as offering a new, demythologized interpretation of the "greatest commandment," placing love of God (the transhuman world) first and foremost in our minds and hearts, with love of our (human) neighbors taking the form of a natural outgrowth and correlate of this love. To love God and neighbor in this demythologized sense is to incline primarily outward to "the vast life and inexhaustible beauty beyond humanity," and turning away from our usual, preponderant focus on interhuman affairs only "so far as need and kindness permit" (CP 4, 420; SP, 721). Achieving a proper balance between these two inclinations is, for Jeffers, not a "slight matter" but is in fact the central challenge of living well—an "essential condition of freedom, and of moral and vital sanity" (CP 4, 419; SP, 720).

Jeffers forthrightly acknowledges that his philosophical inhumanism is out of step with the dominant thrust of modern culture and politics. As we have seen, he believes modern culture has irreversibly entered an era of "civil struggles and emerging Caeserism that binds republics with brittle iron." "Civilization everywhere," he writes, "is in its age of decline and abnormal violence" (CP 4, 420; SP, 721), trends that have only accelerated since Jeffers wrote these words. As we become increasingly massed into warring factions, Jeffers believes many of us will lose our ability to think freely and independently and come to identify with facile, ready-made political identities. At the same time, he believes that the fundamental truths of inhumanism will persist and will be awaiting us on the other side of the agonies and evils of civilizational decline. He believes that "persons who have lost everything, in the culmination of these evils, and stand beyond hope and almost beyond fear" (CP 4, 420–21; SP, 722) may find the basic, permanent truths of inhumanism once again and find a way to rebuild meaningful lives on the other side of the evils that plague our age.

* * *

I return in closing to "other" problem of evil with which I began this study of Jeffers's thought. Having tracked the guiding thread of inhumanist sensibilities, perspectives, and practices that structure Jeffers's mature poetry, we are now better positioned to appreciate how inhumanism might help us approach this problem differently. I should emphasize that I am referring to a different *approach* to the problem of evil rather than a *solution*. I do not think that Jeffers's poetry (or any other mode of thought or practice, for that matter) allows us either to solve or dis-solve this problem; rather I propose that inhumanism allows us to reframe the realities of evil and to address them from an alternative angle. What inhumanism promises is not an end to evil but a particular way of facing and addressing it and of trying to find consolation and reasons for persisting amid its ongoing presence.

We can attain a firmer understanding of the nature of this approach by considering the well-known "whirlwind" speeches in the Book of Job (38:1–42:6), in which God addresses Job's laments at the undeserved injustices he has suffered at the hands of Satan. In an illuminating analysis of these speeches, theologian Kathryn Schifferdecker suggests that what allows Job to move beyond the despair associated with the suffering he undergoes (recall that Job loses all of his possessions and his sons and daughters are killed) is precisely the adoption of an inhuman, radically non-anthropocentric perspective concerning his own life and concerning the place of human beings in the planetary and cosmic schema.[7] Schifferdecker concedes that God's response to Job's laments has often puzzled readers. Rather than trying to explain or justify Job's suffering to him, God takes Job on a cosmic tour of creation, placing particular emphasis on all the things that lie beyond the orbit of human concern and control. When speaking to Job, God appears in general to be most concerned with wild beings and relations that exist largely outside the human orbit. His attention is not primarily focused on the lives of human individuals but is instead directed toward the wildness of inhuman and more-than-human realities. Job is told about: the formation of the earth, the seas, and the stars; the birth of wild mountain goats and the calving of deer; the freedom of the wild ass; the might and courage of the horse; the wild animals who play and feed in the mountains; the strength and size of Behemoth and Leviathan, and so on.

Schifferdecker suggests, though, that human beings are not denied a specific place within God's creation in the whirlwind speeches; rather, our lives are reoriented and reframed, our task and Job's task articulated anew. She writes:

> Humanity has a place […]. in God's creation. It is a place, however, not of dominion, but of humility and of wonder. Job is invited in the whirlwind speeches to expand his vision and to see the world in a new way. He is invited to reorient himself, to understand that he is not the center of the cosmos. He is invited to see the world from God's point of view and to understand anew his place in that world.[8]

---

[7] Kathryn M. Schifferdecker, "Of Stars and Sea Monsters: Creation Theology in the Whirlwind Speeches," *Word & World* 31 (2011): 357–66.

[8] Schifferdecker, "Of Stars and Sea Monsters," 365.

By encouraging us to climb out of the "pit" of humanity, and by providing the conditions whereby we can "uncenter" and "unhumanize" (CP 3, 399; SP, 676) ourselves, Jeffers is attempting to accomplish something very much like the shift in perspective Schifferdecker describes here in regard to Job. To this end, Jeffers does not deny or downplay the difficulties of existence or the sorts of evils that might cause us to despair of life; he acknowledges their presence, even grants them full-throated articulations in his poems. But he places those evils in relation to, and often side-by-side with, the beauty of things—and in so doing recurrently directs our attention to that beauty. The approach to evil that emerges from Jeffers poetry is one in which our suffering and the suffering of other sentient creatures matters, to be sure; but this aspect of the sentient condition is shown to be but one dimension of an extraordinarily varied and rich planetary and cosmic drama.

From an inhumanist perspective, it is entirely reasonable to address and even try to diminish the superfluous and useless evils that characterize our age. Inhumanism doesn't offer, however, childish promises about completely eliminating such suffering or finding a political or religious savior that might bring about a condition that is free from evil. What follows from inhumanism is a rather different picture of life in common. In this picture, we confront and try to delimit useless evils whenever and wherever it is reasonably possible to do so, but not (contra Levinas) because such efforts constitute the ultimate or highest meaning of human existence. We do so instead in order to release ourselves and others to the possibility of contemplating and engaging with the transhuman magnificence of things. It is this latter possibility that creates a worthwhile life and that allows us, like Job, to relocate ourselves anew in the larger cosmic and planetary scheme of things.

Inhumanism thus tries to steer us to an experience of the "deep peace and final joy" (CP 3, 310; SP, 646) that comes from knowing that the more-than-human world is *exorbitant*: that it literally exceeds our orbit, as well as our mastery and understanding. To be sure, the difficulties of existence do not disappear with this lived and felt recognition, but they do take on a different cast and carry a different weight. They are seen as but one part of the fabric of existence, one that calls for response and engagement like all other aspects of existence. Jeffers sometimes seeks (unsuccessfully, to my mind) to find beauty in useless suffering, to give it a place in the grandeur of the whole, and to find consolation thereby. I see no reason to take that particular tack. Affirming life and existence *in toto*, even loving it, does not require us to give up having preferences or removing obstacles that block ourselves and others from living a worthwhile and beautiful life. But it is these sorts of criteria—the preferences for attending to and engaging with things of lasting value and beauty—that primarily frame and give orientation to an inhumanist way of life, not merely the struggle against evils.

An inhumanist way of life and thought staves off despair and life-pessimism by turning us away from the expectation that events should unfold according to our measure and our expectations. It is precisely when real events do not meet our ideal demands, or when our ideal demands do not manifest as real events, that we feel tempted to turn our backs on life and cast aspersions on it. Inhumanism's rejection of this anthropocentric orientation does not, however, yield any hope or optimism about existence; and it certainly has no truck with Leibnizian confidence that this is the best of all possible worlds. Rather, it would have us turn our attention to the magnificence and exorbitance of transhuman existence in the belief that a genuinely worthwhile and beautiful life can be built on the foundation of this turn outward. In making this turn, we are not met by solutions to the problem of evil or transcendent answers to the meaning of existence. Rather what is presented to us are questions and challenges that indicate a way of life and a rule of conduct that can help us make the initial steps beyond the anthropocentric frame: Can we learn to love that which exceeds our measure? Can we live in such a way as to become worthy of the beauty of things? Can we learn to add the beauty of things?

In the final analysis, the inhumanist philosophy of Robinson Jeffers can perhaps be best understood as an invitation to undertake transformative practices aimed at living well. This poetic philosophy marks the opening to a new world amid the collapse and decline of the old. It offers a means of persisting through and beyond the critical limitations that mark our anthropocentric civilization and heritage in view of trying to build something better. It encourages us to create more beautiful lives in view of the astonishing beauty and magnificence of things from which we have emerged and to which we will return. That we have only the briefest stretch of time within which to strive consciously and intentionally toward these aims does nothing to diminish their significance; rather, awareness of our finitude only makes the task more urgent and renders our actions more earnest.

SUGGESTIONS FOR FURTHER READING

Readers who are interested in exploring Jeffers's work at more length are encouraged first of all to read Jeffers's own writings. Both his poetry and prose are approachable for the novice, but they also repay several subsequent re-readings and careful study. A good (and relatively brief) collection of Jeffers's poetry and prose to begin with is the volume edited by Albert Gelpi, *The Wild God of the World: An Anthology of Robinson Jeffers* (Stanford: Stanford University Press, 2003). Gelpi's Introduction to this volume also provides a fine overview of Jeffers's life and work. Readers who desire a larger sampling should turn to Tim Hunt's collection, *The Selected Poetry of Robinson Jeffers*. This work (which I have cited throughout as SP) contains nearly all of Jeffers's most influential lyrics and narratives, and some of his very best prose works as well. Hunt's brief but expert introduction to the volume is essential reading. *The Collected Poetry of Robinson Jeffers*, also edited by Tim Hunt, is the standard scholarly edition of Jeffers's works. The volumes in this collection are listed in full in the "Abbreviations of Works by Robinson Jeffers" and cited throughout this book as CP.

Considerable insight into Jeffers's thought and life can be gleaned from his (and Una's) letters. A short collection of this correspondence, along with a number of photographs by Leigh Wiener, can be found in Anne N. Ridgeway, ed., *The Selected Letters of Robinson Jeffers* (Baltimore: Johns Hopkins University Press, 1968). Readers who want access to more of Jeffers's letters can turn to the exhaustive three-volume set expertly edited by James Karman (these volumes are listed in the "Abbreviations of Works by Robinson Jeffers" and cited throughout this book as CL).

In terms of secondary literature on Jeffers's work, I recommend the beginner start with either of James Karman's two splendid introductory books: *Robinson Jeffers: Poet of California* (Brownsville, OR: Story Line Press, 1995), or *Robinson Jeffers: Poet and Prophet* (Stanford: Stanford University Press, 2015). Karman is a careful scholar and penetrating reader of Jeffers's poetry, but his works are entirely accessible to the non-specialist. An older biographical introduction to Jeffers that is filled with important details about his life and thought is Melba Berry Bennett, *The Stone Mason of Tor House: The Life and Work of Robinson Jeffers* (Los Angeles: The Ward Ritchie Press, 1966).

More advanced critical studies of Jeffers's work that have been influential both in Jeffers's scholarship and for my own reading of Jeffers include: Robert J. Brophy, *Robinson Jeffers: Myth, Ritual, and Symbol in his Narrative Poems* (Cleveland: Case Western Reserve University Press, 1973); William H. Nolte, *Rock and Hawk: Robinson Jeffers and the Romantic Agony* (Athens: University of Georgia Press, 1978); Robert Zaller, *The Cliffs of Solitude: A Reading of Robinson Jeffers* (Cambridge: Cambridge University Press, 1983); William Everson, *The Excesses of God: Robinson Jeffers as a Religious Figure* (Stanford: Stanford University Press, 1988); Robert Zaller, *Robinson Jeffers and the American Sublime* (Stanford: Stanford University Press, 2012); George Hart, *Inventing the Language to Tell It: Robinson Jeffers and the Biology of Consciousness* (New York: Fordham University Press, 2013); Deborah Fleming, *Towers of Myth & Stone: Yeats's Influence on Robinson Jeffers* (Columbia, SC: University of South Carolina Press, 2015); and Geneva Gano, *The Little Art Colony and US Modernism: Carmel, Provincetown, Taos* (Edinburgh: Edinburgh University Press, 2020).

Earlier works on Jeffers's inhumanism from which I have profited include Mercedes Cunningham Monjian, *Robinson Jeffers: A Study in Inhumanism* (Pittsburgh: University of Pittsburgh Press, 1958), and Arthur B. Coffin, *Robinson Jeffers: Poet of Inhumanism* (Madison: University of Wisconsin Press, 1971). Finally, there are several excellent collections of essays that will give readers a fuller sense of the various scholarly approaches to reading Jeffers, including James Karman, ed., *Critical Essays on Robinson Jeffers* (Boston, MA: G. K. Hall & Co., 1990); Robert Zaller, ed., *Centennial Essays for Robinson Jeffers* (Newark: University of Delaware Press, 1991); Robert Brophy, ed., *Robinson Jeffers: Dimensions of a Poet* (New York: Fordham University Press, 1995); and ShaunAnne Tangney, ed., *The Wild That Attracts Us: New Critical Essays on Robinson Jeffers*, (Albuquerque, NM: University of New Mexico Press, 2015).

INDEX

Agamben, Giorgio 66
"age of tyrants" 25
ancient philosophical schools 6, 26
"ancient quarrel" 3
"Answer, The" (Jeffers) 88
"antennae of the race" 24
Anthropocene 1, 76–80
anthropocentrism 6, 46, 73
anthropogenic 30
anthropological difference 11–12, 73
anthropological machine 66–67
"Apology for Bad Dreams" (Jeffers) 19, 29, 33, 68
Augustine 20

Bacchae (Euripides) 64–66, 86
Barclay, Reverend 21, 42–43, 57
Baudelaire, Charles 1
beauty 26, 29–30, 32, 52, 54–56, 62, 66, 68, 72–73, 86–87, 91, 96, 105
Berkeley, George 57
"Birds and Fishes" (Jeffers) 33
"Blind Horses" (Jeffers) 41
"Boats in a Fog" (Jeffers) 90
"Broken Balance, The" (Jeffers) 27

Cadmus 64–65
Capitalocene 78
Carson, Rachel 56
Cawdor (Jeffers) 64
Civilization and Its Discontents (Freud) 35
collective immaturity 100, 102
collective introversion 101
Commins, Saxe 99
Consolation of Philosophy, The (Boethius) 37
"Contemplation of the Sword" (Jeffers) 25
"Continent's End" (Jeffers) 51
cosmos: "as if for the first time" 51–55; beholding truth 55–60; inhuman virtues 60–62; nature of things 47–51

Crutzen, Paul 77
"Cycle, The" (Jeffers) 29

Darwin, Charles 14, 38, 68, 101
De rerum natura (Lucretius Carus) 47, 60, 68
"De rerum virtute" (Jeffers) 60, 62, 70
Deleuze, Gilles 14, 76
Descent of Man, The (Darwin) 68
Deus sive Natura (Spinoza) 43
Dionysus 64–66, 86–87
Double Axe and Other Poems, The (Jeffers) 99–100

early life and conversion, Jeffers 6–11
Eliot, T. S. 2
Empedocles 3
ethico-aesthetic 73
Euripides 63–64, 66
"Evening Ebb" (Jeffers) 54
evil 19–20; natural evil 29–32; problem of 20–23; the sword 24–29

"Fire on the Hills" (Jeffers) 31
freedom 43, 89, 97–98
Freud, Sigmund 35–36, 38, 42, 44

"Give Your Heart to the Hawks" (Jeffers) 30
Greek tragedy 63
Grosz, Elizabeth 14–15
Guattari, Félix 76

Hadot, Pierre 5–6
Haraway, Donna 13
hexameters 2–3
Homo sapiens 74, 76, 78
honest atheism 22
Hubble, Edwin 49
human interests 30
human narcissism 38

human society 11
human souls 48
human vulnerability 35
humanism: on anthropocen(e)trism 76–80; anthropological machine 66–67; becoming something other than human 73–76; great frame 71–73; human dawn 67–70; tragedy 63–66
"Humanist's Tragedy, The" (Jeffers) 64, 66, 86
Hunt, Tim 94

idealism 57–58
immanent frame 22, 33
inhuman existence 14–15
inhuman virtues 60–62
inhumanism 11–15, 46, 100–101, 103, 105–6
"Inhumanist, The" (Jeffers) 68
"Intellectuals" (Jeffers) 40, 43–44
inter-human order 23

Jeffries, Richard 56
Job 104–5
Judeo-Christian tradition 38, 43

Kant, Immanuel 58, 75

large-scale civilizations 42, 95
Levinas, Emmanuel 22–24, 26
literary theory 2
Lucretian Epicureanism 48
Lucretius Carus, Titus 3, 47–48, 55–56, 60, 68
Luhan, Mabel Dodge 28
Lyotard, Jean-François 12–13

"Manifesto for Cyborgs, A" (Haraway) 13
"Margrave" (Jeffers) 50, 92
mass society 27–28
"Measure, The" (Jeffers) 48, 50
"Meditation on Saviors" (Jeffers) 44
memoria technica 72
modern civilizations 36
modern humanity 25
modernity 1, 24
molar species 76
"Monument" (Jeffers) 71
more-than-human world 6, 12, 15, 24, 30, 44, 56, 67, 70–71, 73, 79–80, 83–84, 100, 102–3

Natura naturans (Spinoza) 44
natural evil 29–33
"New Mexican Mountain" (Jeffers) 28
Nietzsche, Friedrich 3, 22, 37–38, 71, 74–75
"Nova" (Jeffers) 52

oeuvre (Jeffers) 22, 30, 63
"Oh Lovely Rock" (Jeffers) 54–55
On the Genealogy of Morality (Nietzsche) 74
"Orca" (Jeffers) 70
Oresteia (Aeschylus) 84
Origin of Species (Darwin) 68
"Original Sin" 68–69, 72

Parmenides 2
Pentheus 64–67, 76, 86
perspectivalism 59
Plato 3–4
Plumwood, Val 93
"Point Pinos and Point Lobos" (Jeffers) 36
postmodernism 12
Pound, Ezra 2

"Quia Absurdum" (Jeffers) 39

"Real World Around Us, The" (Carson) 56
religion 35, 38, 42
Republic (Plato) 3–4
"Return" (Jeffers) 60
"Roan Stallion" (Jeffers) 81, 83
rock-solid themes 1, 4
Rolland, Romain 35
Rossetti, Dante Gabriel 8
rule of conduct 102, 106

"Salmon Fishing" (Jeffers) 30
savannah hypothesis 69n7
saviors 35–36; beyond civilization, beyond saviors 36–42; beyond individual 42–45
Schifferdecker, Kathryn 104–5
"Shine, Perishing Republic" (Jeffers) 89
"Sign-Post" (Jeffers) 87
Socrates 3–4
spiritual exercises 5
"Steelhead, Wild Pig, the Fungus" (Jeffers) 31
Stoermer, Eugene 77
superfluous evils 27

Tamar (Jeffers) 10
"Theory of Truth" (Jeffers) 57
Thus Spoke Zarathustra (Nietzsche) 37
Tor House 29, 32
totalitarianism 22–23
"Tower Beyond Tragedy, The" (Jeffers) 72, 83
"Trap, The" (Jeffers) 27
truth 16, 39, 42, 56–60, 65

useless suffering 26, 30, 105

value: breaking mold 83–88; dying well 92–94; earnest lives 88–92; inhumanism and politics 94–98; obscuring human fidelity 81–83
Vardamis, Alex 45
virtus 60–61, 71
"Vulture" (Jeffers) 93

"Wheel of Fortune" (Jeffers) 37, 52, 89, 95
"Women at Point Sur, The" (Jeffers) 21, 42–43, 57

www.ingramcontent.com/pod-product-compliance
Ingram Content Group UK Ltd.
Pitfield, Milton Keynes, MK11 3LW, UK
UKHW042344220426
470291UK00001B/31